Neven Maguire's
Home Economics *for* Life

NEVEN MAGUIRE'S HOME ECONOMICS for LIFE

GILL BOOKS

Gill Books
Hume Avenue
Park West
Dublin 12
www.gillbooks.ie

Gill Books is an imprint of M.H. Gill and Co.

978 07171 8079 0

Compiled by Orla Broderick
Designed by grahamthew.com
Photography: Joanne Murphy (joanne-murphy.com), assisted by Deborah Ryan
Food styling: Johan van der Merwe (foodstylistjohan.com), assisted by Chloe Chan, James Butler, Ciara Altman and Clodagh Dunphy
Edited by Kristin Jensen
Indexed by Eileen O'Neill
Printed in Italy by L.E.G.O. SpA

This book is typeset in 10.5 on 13pt Minion Pro.
The paper used in this book comes from the wood pulp of managed forests. For every tree felled, at least one tree is planted, thereby renewing natural resources.

A CIP catalogue record for this book is available from the British Library.

5 4 3 2 1

Dedication

For the many wonderful staff who have worked with us over the years in MacNean House & Restaurant. Thank you for your hard work, loyalty, support and friendship.

Acknowledgements

Writing this book has been an enriching, and at times emotional, experience. It has taken me back to the beginning, discovering all over again the pleasure you get from cooking good food well. Not everyone is going to be a chef, but I still firmly believe that everyone should be able to do the basics, and do them well. Some people will develop an interest and get a lifetime of pleasure from their time spent in the kitchen – as will their family and friends.

Some of these recipes took me back to my mother's first lessons, to my time spent in Fermanagh Catering College, and to distant nights when we cooked for very few guests wondering how we would keep the doors open. My parents did not have it easy. My dad, Joe, would be astonished and delighted by how much Irish food culture has developed over the years. My mum, Vera, was with us as the restaurant grew in popularity and awards came our way. She was very proud that she was there from day one.

To bring this book to you involves a lot of talented, hard-working people, many of whom have been with me for several years. A very special thank you to Nicki Howard who commissions and comes up with many of the ideas. I just love working with you. Orla Broderick has compiled the recipes once again. This book would not have been possible without your help. It is a pleasure to work with Catherine Gough and Teresa Daly of Gill Books. Thanks to Johan van der Merwe, who styled the food, and my right-hand woman, Claire Beasley, another superb job. To Chloe Chan and James Butler, thank you for ensuring each dish looked and tasted delicious. I am delighted again with the way Joanne Murphy photographs food. Thanks again to Kristin Jensen for another great editing job. And a big thank you to all of the staff in MacNean who are on hand to help, including my wife Amelda, Restaurant Manager Bláthin McCabe, Assistant Manager Aidan Kelly, Head Chef Carmel McGirr, Sous Chef Olivia Raftery, and the ever patient Andrea Doherty who coordinates everyone so efficiently.

Throughout the year there are many people I work with that I hugely appreciate. Days spent with Diarmuid Murphy, Daragh Lawless and Shauna Walsh working on Simply Better are a pleasure. And thank you to the many staff I meet in Dunnes, and to Mrs Heffernan and Anne Heffernan for making it possible. Thanks also to Maria Hickey, President of the Association of Teachers of Home Economics. I'm proud to be your ambassador. And I couldn't go without thanking my very own Home Economics teacher, Mairead McMorrow.

It was another good year filming for RTÉ and Brian Walsh, with David Hare and our trusty crew of Billy Keady and Ray de Brún. And thank you to TVPR for letting everyone know when we are on TV. Bord Bia have been an immense help to us, thank you Hylda Adams and Tara McCarty.

I love meeting people at demos and working with my brother Kenneth who has his own business running demos at festivals up and down the country. Thank you to John Rooney and Eoin O'Flynn of Flogas for continued support.

Thank you to Marty Whelan and Sinead Wylde for putting up with me every Friday morning on LyricFM, and to Marian Finucane and her Radio 1 team. It is always a pleasure to be on your show. To everyone in the *Farmer's Journal*, especially Mairead Lavery for always believing in me. I enjoy writing for your paper every week.

Media matters are handled by my agent, John Masterson, and his team at Purcell Masterson, Bridget O'Dea, Sally Leadbetter, Mary Tallent, Anne Ryder and Dean Egan.

The biggest thank you is reserved for my wife Amelda. She knows how much I appreciate her but, like many lucky men, we need to tell our loved ones how important they are more often than we do!

Contents

INTRODUCTION

Did you know that I was the first boy in my secondary school to study Home Economics? I certainly got teased for it at the time, but it was the foundation for what has become a life-long passion. In fact, my first ever cookery demonstration was in my Home Economics class (I still remember it was smoked salmon and leek tart) and now I do hundreds of demonstrations all over the country every year!

As a nation we've come a long way since then, and now Home Economics is the most popular extracurricular subject in Belvedere College, whose Home Economics classrooms I had the privilege to open a few years ago. Home Economics teachers up and down the country instill such important life skills in the next generation every day. I am so inspired by the work they do that I am delighted to be an ambassador for the Association of Teachers of Home Economics.

However, I believe that Home Economics isn't just for the classroom! Just as teachers encourage parents to help in the development of their child's reading and writing at home, shouldn't we as parents also sow the seeds for a love of cooking? After all, our children will grow into adults who will have to feed themselves – and their families – every day. Wouldn't it be fantastic if by the time your child is ready to leave home – for college or elsewhere – they had the basics in their repertoire from which they can build a life-long love of good food?

As I have seen from meeting people every day, it's not just children who want to learn. Many adults find themselves going back to school to learn a skill they never had the chance to learn until now. I firmly believe that everyone should have the opportunity to learn the pleasure of sourcing, preparing and cooking great food. And it's never too late to start.

So this book is an invitation to join me on this journey and cook the book from beginning to end! Why not aim to learn one recipe per week? By the time you get to the end, you will have learned and mastered what I believe are the 50 most important recipes for life.

You'll discover how to make a good tomato sauce, how to dress a salad, roasting techniques and how to make stock from the bones, the art of brown bread, the trick for perfect scrambled eggs, formulas for sauces and soups and, of course, a comforting chocolate cake. You'll cook more, waste less and gain a whole lot more pleasure from your kitchen in the process.

The recipes in this book pass on to you everything that I've learned – from cooking with my mother, Vera, and in Home Economics classes at secondary school, to working in restaurant kitchens around the world – broken down into easy-to-follow, step-by-step bites.

So let's go back to school together to learn and enjoy Home Economics for life!

THE EQUIPMENT

The first step to learning how to cook is to get the right equipment. You don't need a lot of gear, but it makes sense to buy the best you can afford so that it will last a decent amount of time. Below are the essential items that everyone who wants to cook

regularly should own, while the nice to have are the things you can build up on. You might choose to buy only some of these, but I like to have them all to hand as they save me time and effort and help me to cook well.

THE ESSENTIALS

Knives (sharpening steel, paring knife, cook's knife and bread/serrated carving knife) – a good carbonated steel brand

Rubber spatulas (heatproof)

Whisks (large and small metal balloon)

Set of heavy-based saucepans (small, medium and large)

Griddle pan (cast iron with metal handle, such as Le Creuset)

Roasting trays (robust, small and large)

Baking sheet (robust, large)

Large non-stick frying pan

Large casserole (cast iron, aluminium or stainless steel)

Metal tongs (ideally with silicone heads)

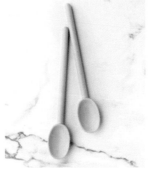

Wooden spoons and spatulas (I use heatproof Matfer Exoglass spoons)

Nest of mixing bowls (Pyrex)

Large measuring jug (Pyrex)

Potato masher

Fish slice

Slotted spoon

Ladle

Pastry brush

Chopping board (thick wooden one for general use and small plastic ones for smellier jobs)

Weighing scales (Salter digital scales)

THE ESSENTIALS CONT.

Set of measuring spoons

Sieve (one coarse, one fine)

Box grater

Rolling pin

Tin opener

Speed vegetable peeler (swivel)

Large colander

Cupcake tin

NICE TO HAVE

Food processor (Magimix is the best brand for a domestic kitchen)

Hand-held blender (my preference is Bamix, but Bosch is a good high street brand)

Wok

Steamer (or an insert tier for a saucepan)

NICE TO HAVE CONT.

Palette knife

Lemon juicer

Lemon zester

Kitchen scissors

Microplane grater (try to build up a selection of different blades)

6 ramekins (try to build up a selection of different sizes)

Fluted round cutters (also with straight-sided edge and in various sizes)

Disposable piping bags and nozzles

Loose-bottomed cake tins (various sizes)

Potato ricer

Flour dredger

Mandolin

Pestle and mortar

THE LARDER

I've kept this to just six main items that I consider to be basic essentials. I use most of them every day and think they're worth always having to hand. With these six items alone it's easy to whip up a quick meal such as an omelette or poached eggs, so you'll never go hungry.

Butter: Irish, of course, from grass-fed cows, as there is no better flavour. Salted butter is a great all-purpose butter to spread on bread or to use in cooking. There is nothing like its richness when you bake.

Flour: A store cupboard staple. I normally have plain and self-raising flour in the house, but I also often use strong white flour for bread and wholemeal flour for soda.

Oil: Rapeseed and extra virgin olive oil. I use rapeseed oil for cooking, unless it's an Italian dish where I think that the flavour of olive oil will work better, and I use extra virgin olive oil for dressings and for finishing dishes. Sometimes a more bland oil is worth using, such as a vegetable or sunflower oil, as they will impart very little of their own flavour and are cheaper, so they're better to use for deep-frying.

Sea salt and black pepper: I like to use a fine sea salt for cooking and occasionally use the more expensive sea salt flakes (Achill Island Sea Salt is a great Irish brand), which have an excellent flavour. I keep a pepper mill filled up with black pepper-corns, although many supermarkets now stock disposable mills.

Eggs: Try to always use free-range or organic eggs, as the flavour is so much better with very little price increase.

Lemons and limes: I couldn't imagine a world without lemons, or limes for that matter, particu-larly when I'm making Asian dishes. I find it's best to store them in a salad drawer in the fridge.

HOW TO PREPARE VEGETABLES

Always shake or brush off loose earth before washing. With the exception of mushrooms, all vegetables must be thoroughly washed before cooking. Brush or wipe mushrooms using a pastry brush. As they are grown in sterile soil, this is sufficient. If they are genuinely wild, then trim them down accordingly and brush or wipe as before.

Vegetables with inedible skins, such as onions, squashes and thick-skinned roots and tubers, need to be peeled. A vegetable peeler or small paring knife is best for peeling. A really sharp knife and a good heavy chopping board are essential for slicing and chopping.

Once peeled the vegetables begin to lose their vitamins, so try not to prepare them hours in advance and leave them soaking in water.

HOW TO PEEL GARLIC

Cut the root end off the clove of garlic. Lie the clove flat on the chopping board and rest the blade of a large knife flat horizontally on it. Lean heavily on the flat blade with the heel of your hand. The garlic clove will crack under the weight and will simultaneously be released from its papery skin. Remove any green stalk from the centre and discard it. Finely chop the clove using a rocking motion.

HOW TO CHOP AN ONION

If you do it this way, you'll get perfect results every time! Peel the onion and chop off the root and tip. (If you're less confident, you can leave the root attached until the last minute to hold the pieces securely together, but don't forget to remove it before cooking!) Cut the onion in half through the root end. Place one half of the onion flat side down on the chopping board. Make about six parallel cuts downwards with the knife tip pointing towards the root end, but not cutting the short root end so that the onion continues to hold together.

Next, with the onion still facing downwards and holding it steady from the root end, make three horizontal cuts, one above the other, towards the root. Again, be careful not to slice all the way through – the half must still hold together at the root.

Finally, finely chop down repeatedly across the width of the onion. Perfect cubes will fall from your knife. It's that easy!

HOW TO CHOP HERBS

Use your cook's knife on a chopping board. Place the herbs in a mound. Holding the top of the knife with one hand, chop back and forth in a rocking motion until finely chopped. Basil is a very delicate herb, so prepare it at the last minute and either tear or shred the leaves so that they don't get too damaged.

Eggs

OMELETTE
SERVES 1

2 large eggs

1 tbsp snipped fresh chives

1 tsp rapeseed oil

a small knob of butter

sea salt and freshly ground black pepper

A well-cooked omelette has to be one of the simplest and quickest meals. Once you have mastered the basic technique you can start adding fillings, such as a sprinkling of grated cheese and/or some chopped cooked ham. A combination of sautéed mixed mushrooms, such as shiitake, oyster and chanterelle, which most supermarkets are now stocking, would make this into a special meal along with some lightly dressed rocket on the side. For me, the perfect omelette is one just tinged with golden brown on the surface and very soft and squidgy on the inside.

Break the eggs into a bowl, then add the chives and season with salt and pepper. Gently beat the eggs with a fork until the yolks and whites are just combined. Don't be tempted to over-beat at this stage, as it will spoil the texture. If anything, under-beating rather than over-beating the eggs seems to make a fluffier omelette.

Place a frying pan with a base that's about 15cm (6in) in diameter on a medium heat. Add the oil and butter. As soon as the butter melts, quickly swirl it around, tilting the pan so that the base and sides get coated. Now turn up the heat to its highest setting.

When the butter is foaming, pour in the beaten egg mixture, tilting it around to spread the eggs in an even layer across the base of the pan. Place on the heat for 5 seconds, then tilt the pan to a 45 degree angle and, using a tablespoon, draw the mixture from the sides to the centre as it sets. Any remaining liquid egg will fill the space. Now turn the pan back the other way and do the same thing. Continue tilting backwards and forwards, pulling the edges with a spoon, until there is only a small amount of the liquid egg left, just on the surface – all this will take no more than 30 seconds. →

Now it's time to start folding. If you're using any fillings, add them now. Tilt the pan again and flip one side of the omelette into the centre, then fold again. You can use a palette knife to help you do this, but I normally never bother. Take the pan to the warm plate and the last fold will be when you tip the omelette out onto the plate. It's worth remembering that an omelette will continue cooking, even on the plate, so serve it immediately.

NEVEN'S TOP TIP

Have everything ready before you begin cooking: bowl, eggs, herbs, frying pan, fork, wooden spatula, salt and pepper, butter and oil. It's also worth putting a plate in a warm oven.

1

POACHED EGGS
SERVES 4

2 tsp white wine vinegar

4 eggs

sea salt and freshly ground black pepper

TO SERVE

hot buttered toast, crispy bacon or baked beans

The key to a good poached egg is to use eggs that are as fresh as possible, although adding vinegar to the water encourages the protein to coagulate more quickly. This means that the whites firm up faster and it also prevents them from dispersing in the water. You can tell how fresh an egg is by putting it in a glass of water – if it lies horizontally at the bottom, it's very fresh; if it starts to float or stand on end, it's less fresh. It's also very important to keep the water at a bare simmer throughout the cooking and not to salt the water, as that may break up the egg white.

Bring a large pan with 2.25 litres (4 pints) of water to a bare simmer, then add the white wine vinegar. Don't add any salt, as this may break up the egg white. The water needs to be at least 5cm (2in) deep to give the poached eggs a good shape.

Break each egg into a teacup or ramekin, as this makes it easier to slide it into the pan. Use a whisk or a spoon to quickly stir the water in one direction until it's all smoothly spinning around like a gentle whirlpool. This helps the white to wrap around the yolk. Gently slide the egg into the water where it's bubbling in the centre. Repeat with the rest of the eggs, then carefully move the pan to the edge of the heat and simmer gently for 3 minutes, until all the whites look set.

Remove each poached egg with a slotted spoon and drain well on a plate lined with kitchen paper. If liked, trim off any straggly bits of white.

Arrange on plates and season with salt and pepper, then serve with some hot buttered toast. Poached eggs are also delicious with crispy bacon or baked beans also make an excellent combination. →

Poached eggs can be prepared up to 24 hours in advance, as they will sit perfectly happily in the fridge. Simply remove the poached eggs with a slotted spoon and plunge into a bowl of iced water. When cold, trim down any ragged ends from the cooked egg white. When ready to use, bring a large pan of water to the boil. Add the poached eggs and cook for 1–2 minutes to warm them through.

1

2

3

4

5

SOFTLY SCRAMBLED EGGS
SERVES 2

6 large eggs

3 tbsp milk or cream

1 tbsp snipped fresh chives (optional)

25g (1oz) butter

sea salt and freshly ground black pepper

TO SERVE

slices of buttered brown soda bread (page 217), toast or bagels

roasted cherry tomatoes on the vine (page 167) (optional)

Soft clouds of perfectly scrambled eggs are one of life's joys and once you have mastered the art of allowing them to finish cooking off the heat, you will never have a problem. If you want to serve more people or if they are going to be part of a bigger breakfast, just multiply the ingredients accordingly. I love them with some smoked salmon or roasted cherry tomatoes on the vine. The method always remains the same, but obviously the larger the quantity, the longer they will take to cook. If eggs are going to be the star of the show, then I'd always try to use free-range or organic and you'll find that there is very little difference in the price. Use cream instead of milk for a richer, creamier finish.

Break the eggs into a bowl and add the milk or cream and plenty of freshly ground black pepper. Blitz with a hand-held blender, as this helps to make the resulting scrambled eggs even lighter and fluffier. Stir in the chives (if using).

Heat a heavy-based saucepan over a medium heat. Add half of the butter and swirl it around so that the base and up the sides of the pan are lightly coated with it. Once the butter has melted and is foaming, add the egg mixture. Using a wooden fork or a wooden spatula, start stirring briskly using backwards and forwards movements all through the egg mixture, making sure that you get right into the corners of the pan to prevent it from sticking. This should take no more than 2–3 minutes.

Once three-quarters of the egg mixture is a creamy, solid mass and a quarter is still liquid, remove the pan from the heat, as they will continue to cook. Add the rest of the butter and continue scrambling with the spatula. The eggs will carry on cooking in the heat from the pan. As soon as there is no liquid left, check the seasoning and add a pinch of salt if you think it needs it. →

Serve the softly scrambled eggs absolutely immediately with some slices of buttered soda bread, toast or bagels and roasted cherry tomatoes on the vine, if liked.

NEVEN'S TOP TIP

Make sure you don't start with the heat too high or you'll end up with rubbery eggs. And whatever you do, once you're cooking the scrambled eggs, don't turn the heat up – just be patient and keep scrambling away. The trick is to remove the pan from the heat while there is still about a quarter of the liquid left, as this will disappear into a creamy mass as you serve the eggs.

1

4

2

3

5

6

PANCAKES
MAKES
ABOUT 8

100g (4oz) plain flour

2 large eggs

300ml (½ pint) milk

1 tbsp sunflower oil

about 25g (1oz) butter

TO SERVE

2–3 tbsp caster sugar

1 lemon, halved and pips removed

The most important piece of kitchen equipment that you need to make perfect pancakes every time is a really good non-stick frying pan, as it makes flipping so much easier. Make sure your frying pan is properly heated before you start cooking too. You can test this by putting a small spoonful of the batter into the frying pan – it should turn golden on the bottom after about 30 seconds.

Put the flour, eggs, milk and sunflower oil in a bowl and whisk to a smooth batter. Leave it to rest for 30 minutes if time allows, but up to two days is fine, covered with cling film in the fridge – just give it a good stir before using, and if you find it has thickened up a little, then loosen it with a splash of milk. But if you're in a hurry, you can cook the pancakes straight away. Leaving the batter to rest allows the starch to absorb the liquid and the air bubbles to disperse, resulting in a pancake that is more even in texture.

Place a medium non-stick frying pan over a medium heat and smear with a tiny knob of butter. Once hot, ladle in a thin layer of batter and cook for 1 minute, until golden. Once the pancake is cooked underneath, give the pan a little shake and the pancake should move easily. Tip the pancake to the edge of the frying pan and three, two, one, flip! Remember, practice makes perfect – it's about having a confident flick of the wrist (the same action that you would use when making a stir-fry in a wok). Cook for another 30–60 seconds, keeping the pancakes warm in a low oven as you go. Repeat until all the batter is used up.

To serve, sprinkle each pancake with the sugar, then add a squeeze of lemon and roll up to eat. →

If you'd prefer to make the pancakes in advance, allow them to cool and then layer them up between pieces of parchment or greaseproof paper and wrap in cling film. They will keep happily for two days in the fridge, then reheat later in a low oven or in the microwave. They can also be frozen for up to two months.

1

4

2

3

5

6

Salad

THE SALAD FORMULA

It's difficult to say exactly what ingredients make the perfect salad. By definition, it should be a seasonally evolving mix of the best ingredients available to you, mostly from your salad drawer in the fridge or, better still, freshly picked from the garden or purchased at a farmers market. It should be simultaneously silky, crunchy, clean, sharp and spiked with herbal bursts while the dressing adds its own tangy flourish.

The closest you will get to perfection is to choose an ingredient from each row of pages 22–23. As long as you pick one thing from each group you can't go wrong, so learn the formula and you'll never look back!

To wash the greens, plunge the leaves into a large basin of cold water and give them a swish, then allow a few minutes for sand or dirt to fall to the bottom. Lift the greens from the bowl and shake or spin them dry, then lay them out on kitchen paper if you think that there is any water left. Put into a suitable salad bowl and season lightly with salt and pepper.

Thinly slice the vegetables into bite-sized chunks, then add the crunch ingredient. Season with salt and pepper, then dress the salad (see page 197 for a dressing recipe), tossing lightly to coat, using the tips of your fingers. Your hands make the best salad tossing tools (for more info, see page 24 on how to dress a salad). Gently pick the herbs off their stalks and roughly tear on top or snip in chives with a scissors. Crumble or tear the cheese into small pieces and scatter on top. Serve immediately, straight to the table.

NEVEN'S TOP TIP

I know that ready-prepared salad leaves in bags are really convenient, but how often have you gone to an open bag to find that the rest of it has wilted and died a death? Try to get into the habit of choosing a few different lettuce heads and making up your own salad mix once a week. Store them in an airtight plastic container with a piece of damp kitchen paper on top or ziplock bag to ensure they stay fresh or consider growing some in a large pot on the patio during the summer months.

CRISP

Romaine lettuce

Little Gem lettuce

Batavia (Lollo Biondo) lettuce

Bag of classic crispy salad

SOFT

Buttterhead lettuce

Red oakleaf lettuce

Lamb's lettuce

Watercress

VEGETABLES

Tomatoes

Cucumber

Avocado

Radishes

Fennel

CRUNCH

Toasted mixed seeds

Toasted pine nuts

Croutons

Crispy bacon lardons

HERBS

Fresh chives

Fresh basil

Fresh flat-leaf parsley

Fresh rocket

CHEESE

Feta

Buffalo mozzarella

Parmesan

Cashel Blue

HOW TO DRESS A SALAD

We all know how important it is to eat plenty of fruit and vegetables, so making a salad instead of cooked vegetables for your dinner is a great option. However, it needs to taste absolutely delicious, which is where your salad dressing comes in. The good news is that your body can absorb far more nutrients from salads with the presence of oil and acid in the salad dressing.

A good salad should be light, bright and full of life, so make sure that your salad leaves are completely dry. Once they are in the bowl, season them with salt and pepper. It's not enough to just season the dressing – a good salad is all about creating layers of flavour.

The best way to dress a salad is to drizzle over just enough dressing to coat the leaves. Adding too much will create a soggy mess and too little will leave something to be desired. Add the dressing little by little, tasting as you go, to make sure you have the perfect amount. See page 197 for a simple salad dressing recipe.

The best tool you can use for dressing a salad is your hands. This ensures that the salad stays light and airy and is handled with a gentle touch. Using your hands to toss allows air to get into the layers and incorporates your ingredients in a more distributed way.

The best way to toss a salad is to drizzle the salad dressing along the walls of your bowl, then lightly toss the greens until the dressing is evenly distributed, resulting in no bruised or crushed leaves. I find it works best to add some of the heavy ingredients for the toss, like the vegetables and crunch ingredient, then add the herbs so that their delicate flavour can shine through more than when they're simply scattered on the top. Finish with the cheese so that your guests get to see what's in the salad and it doesn't all sink to the bottom. And there you have it – a perfectly dressed salad!

TOMATO AND MOZZARELLA SALAD
SERVES 4

675g (1½lb) tomatoes of different shapes and sizes, including some slightly under-ripe more acidic varieties if possible (see introduction)

extra virgin olive oil

250g (9oz) buffalo mozzarella

1 sprig of fresh basil

sea salt and freshly ground black pepper

TO SERVE

sourdough or crusty rustic bread

Also known as a Caprese salad, this Italian classic appears on menus everywhere, but very few places make it well. Of course, this is normally down to the ingredients. In Italy this is often made with semi-green tomatoes, which have a higher acidity then a ripe red tomato. Buffalo mozzarella is quite rich, so the best balance of different colours and varieties is ideal if you can find them. It's also worth looking out for fresh Genovese basil, which has small leaves and an intensity of fragrance and flavour that makes it almost unrecognisable to the standard sort. Happily, Dunnes Stores often have it as a growing pot that, regularly watered, will last you quite a long time.

Cut the tomatoes into different-sized slices and chunks depending on their size – large misshapen tomatoes often look better cut into cross-sections (cut out the core if it looks tough). Put them in a bowl and sprinkle with sea salt. Set aside for 10 minutes to allow the flavours to develop, then add 1 tablespoon of olive oil and toss gently to combine.

Arrange the tomatoes on a plate or platter, spooning over all their delicious juices. Tear the mozzarella over the top, then tear the basil leaves into small pieces and scatter on top. Drizzle the whole thing with a little more oil and season with a little salt and a good grinding of pepper. Serve with plenty of crusty bread to mop up all of those delicious juices. →

NEVEN'S TOP TIP

Before you start, make sure that all of the ingredients are at room temperature – not that you should be refrigerating your tomatoes or basil anyway. If you find that the tomatoes you have bought are not as ripe as you'd like, put them in your fruit bowl and leave them to ripen in a sunny spot in your kitchen.

1

2

3

4

CHOPPED GREEN SALAD
SERVES 4

1 bunch of spring onions

½ cucumber

2 sprigs of fresh soft herbs, such as flat-leaf parsley or basil

1 ripe avocado

1 cos lettuce

1 tub of cress (optional)

50g (2oz) feta or Cheddar cheese

3 tbsp extra virgin olive oil

1 tbsp red wine vinegar

½ tsp Dijon mustard

sea salt and freshly ground black pepper

It can be very expensive to order a bespoke creation in the trendy delis and salad bars that are happily becoming more widespread around the country, so why not save some money and make your own? Chopped salads are just like regular salads, only with a different presentation – all the ingredients are chopped, greens and all, and incorporated together instead of layered. It's only a minor detail, but one with lots of options. It can also be easily eaten with just a fork so it makes a great packed lunch option, although I'd always bring the dressing separately so that everything stays nice and fresh.

Trim and chop the spring onions and cut the cucumber into slices on a large chopping board. Tear up the herb leaves and put it all in a large pile in the middle of the board, then start chopping until everything is fairly finely chopped.

Cut the avocado in half and remove the stone, then peel off and discard the skin and add the avocado flesh to the board. Tear off the outer leaves of the lettuce and discard them, then add the rest with the cress (if using). Crumble over the cheese and continue chopping and mixing until everything on the board is evenly chopped up into little pieces.

Transfer to a bowl, then drizzle over the oil and vinegar, add the mustard and season with salt and pepper. Mix everything until evenly coated and serve immediately. →

Anyone can make chopped salads – just make sure you use a really good, sharp chef's knife and a nice big chopping board. Chopped salads are a great way to practise your knife skills (see page 000 for more detailed instructions). I normally start with the harder, crunchier vegetables first, but that's up to you. Just be careful not to get too carried away and watch your fingers!

1

Soup

THE SOUP FORMULA

A hug in a bowl is how my late mother, Vera, always described this cold-weather comfort food that makes a delicious meal, particularly when served with a toasted cheese sandwich or some crusty bread rolls. This formula is designed to show you just how easy it is to make a soup without a proper recipe. It works best with starchy vegetables that when cooked and puréed break down and give the soup a lovely creamy consistency. I've suggested some of my favourites, but you can experiment with your own or use a combination, depending on what is available.

It's a good idea to get everything prepped before you start to cook. Peel and finely chop everything you're going to need, so choose ingredients from each row on pages 38–39, for example 150g (5oz) of the aromatic, 2 teaspoons of the flavour add-in, 450g (1lb) of the vegetables and 900ml (1½ pints) of liquid. Think of the formula as a basic 1 + 3 + 6 ratio and you'll never look back.

Heat a good knob of butter or a splash of rapeseed or olive oil in a large pan over a medium heat. Add your chosen aromatic and sauté for about 5 minutes, until softened, tender and translucent. Don't be tempted to rush this step – sautéing breaks down the cell walls in the aromatics, which is crucial for a creamy, smooth finish. Stir in the flavour add-in and cook for 1 minute. Add the vegetables, stirring to combine, then pour in the liquid. Season with salt and pepper and bring to the boil. Reduce the heat and simmer for 15–20 minutes, until the vegetables are completely tender.

Purée the soup with a hand-held blender or in a food processor (in batches if necessary). Season to taste. If you think the soup is too thick, just add a little more liquid until you have reached your desired consistency. Reheat gently, then ladle into warmed bowls and embellish it with a nice garnish (see suggestions below), if liked. Think of it as an opportunity to balance the flavours and textures of a soup and make it more appealing to the eye.

How to jazz up your soup

+ For creaminess and tang, garnish with a dollop of crème fraîche, sour cream or yogurt.

+ Freshly chopped or roughly torn herbs such as parsley, coriander, chives or dill on top bring a welcome contrast.

+ Crunchy bacon crumbled over is always a winner.

+ A sprinkle of croutons or toasted seeds will add a lovely crunch.

+ A little Parmesan or Pecorino will brighten up even the blandest of soups.

+ Thinly sliced fresh chilli or a drizzle of chilli oil will certainly spice thing up.

+ A swirl of your favourite pesto (page 183) will add another layer of flavour. →

If you don't want to go to the trouble of making a stock (see the recipes on page 50 and page 52), a good-quality stock cube is a good option. Water also works well and allows the flavour of the base vegetables to shine, or use a combination of two liquids, such as stock and milk or coconut milk, to give a richer finish.

AROMATICS

Onions   Leeks   Shallots   Celery

FLAVOUR ADD-INS

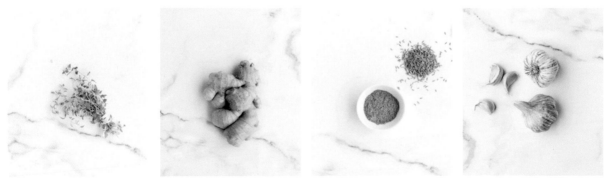

Fresh thyme   Fresh ginger   Ground cumin   Garlic

VEGETABLES

Sweet potatoes

Butternut squash

Carrots

Potatoes

LIQUID

Vegetable stock (page 52)

Chicken stock (page 50)

Milk

Coconut milk

CREAMY VEGETABLE SOUP
SERVES 4–6

Everyone should know how to make a good, simple soup. The key to this type of soup is cooking the vegetables for the shortest amount of time that they need in order to be soft enough to be blended. Traditionally this type of soup would have used flour as a thickener, but I have found that people are increasingly looking for a gluten-free option.

25g (1oz) butter

1 large onion, finely chopped

1 garlic clove, crushed

500g (18oz) peas (or sliced mushrooms, sweetcorn or baby spinach)

750ml (1¼ pints) chicken or vegetable stock (page 50 or 52)

150ml (¼ pint) cream

25g (1oz) mature Cheddar, Parmesan, Pecorino or Gruyère cheese, grated

sea salt and freshly ground black pepper

chopped fresh flat-leaf parsley, to garnish

TO SERVE

brown soda bread (see page 217)

Melt the butter in a large pan over a medium heat. Add the onion and garlic and cook for about 5 minutes, stirring, until softened but not coloured. Add the vegetables of your choice and stock and bring to the boil. Season with salt and pepper, then reduce the heat and simmer for 10 minutes, until the vegetables are completely soft.

Stir the cream into the soup and blitz with a hand-held blender or in a food processor (in batches if necessary) until smooth. Stir in the cheese, then reheat gently until hot but not boiling. Season to taste.

Ladle the soup into warmed bowls and scatter over the parsley to garnish. Add a good grinding of black pepper to each one and serve with some brown soda bread. →

This soup can be made ahead and kept in the fridge for two or three days or it freezes very well for up to one month. Ladle single portions into ziplock bags so that you always have a quick meal option at the ready.

1

2

3

4

THAI BROTH WITH PAK CHOI
SERVES 6–8

This is a spicy and refreshing broth that is found on the menu of all Thai restaurants. I was taught how to cook it while on holiday in Thailand with my wife, Amelda. This one is made with prawns but it's also delicious made with 200g (7oz) of boneless, skinless chicken that has been thinly sliced.

600ml (1 pint) chicken stock (page 50)

2 x 400ml (14fl oz) tins of coconut milk (preferably Thai Gold)

juice of 1 lime

50g (2oz) shiitake mushrooms, thinly sliced

20g (¾oz) fresh galangal, peeled and sliced

3 fresh or dried kaffir lime leaves

2 lemongrass stalks, trimmed and chopped

2 tbsp Thai fish sauce (nam pla)

1 tbsp sweet chilli sauce

2 tsp tomato purée

1 tsp light brown sugar

1–2 crushed dried bird's eye chillies

200g (7oz) raw peeled king prawns

1 head of pak choi, thinly sliced

a good handful of fresh coriander leaves, to garnish

chilli oil, for drizzling

Heat the stock in a pan. Add the coconut milk, lime juice, mushrooms, galangal, lime leaves, lemongrass, fish sauce, sweet chilli sauce, tomato purée, brown sugar and dried chillies to taste. Bring to the boil, stirring to combine, then reduce the heat and simmer for 5 minutes. Taste and adjust as you think necessary – you may think it needs a little extra of something.

Pass the soup through a fine-mesh sieve into a clean pan. Add the prawns and pak choi and bring back to the boil, then reduce the heat and simmer gently for about 5 minutes, until the prawns and vegetables are cooked through.

Ladle into warmed deep bowls and garnish with coriander and a drizzle of chilli oil – the amount you add depends on how you spicy you like your food. →

Thai fish sauce (nam pla) is used to season the soup instead of salt and pepper, but make sure you buy a good-quality one, such as Thai Gold or the Squid brand, as some of the less authentic versions are extremely salty.

CHUNKY VEGETABLE SOUP
SERVES 4–6

50g (2oz) pearl barley

2 tbsp rapeseed oil

1 onion, diced

1 carrot, diced

1 small leek, diced

2 celery sticks, diced

1 tsp chopped fresh thyme

50g (2oz) rindless streaky bacon or raw chorizo, diced (optional)

1.2 litres (2 pints) chicken or vegetable stock (page 50 or 52)

1 tbsp chopped fresh flat-leaf parsley

sea salt and freshly ground black pepper

TO SERVE

brown soda bread (page 217)

When the weather gets cold, this is the soup I crave. It's actually very healthy and brimming with goodness, but it certainly won't leave you feeling deprived either. It really is a very flexible recipe and you can omit the barley if you are coeliac or substitute with brown rice if you prefer. Sometimes I add a sprinkling of cayenne pepper to give it a kick.

Put the pearl barley in a sieve and rinse well under cold running water.

Heat the rapeseed oil in a pan over a medium heat. Stir in the onion, carrot, leek, celery and thyme. Add the bacon or chorizo (if using) and sauté for 5 minutes, until the vegetables are softened and the bacon or chorizo is sizzling.

Pour the stock into the pan, add the rinsed barley and bring to the boil, then reduce the heat and simmer for about 20 minutes, until the vegetables and barley are completely tender but still holding their shape. Stir in the parsley and season to taste.

To serve, ladle the soup into warmed bowls and hand around a separate basket of soda bread. →

NEVEN'S TOP TIP

If you want to make this soup even more substantial, add some cooked diced chicken or leftover diced roast beef to it at the very end of the cooking time when you are adding the parsley. Otherwise a drained and rinsed tin of your favourite beans or pulses is a good addition too.

1

2

CHICKEN STOCK
MAKES ABOUT 1.2 LITRES (2 PINTS)

1 large raw or cooked chicken carcass, skin and fat removed

2 leeks, trimmed and chopped

2 onions, chopped

2 carrots, chopped

2 celery sticks, chopped

1 sprig of fresh thyme

1 bay leaf

a handful of fresh parsley stalks

1 tsp white peppercorns

Chicken stock is the secret ingredient of restaurant food. A good chicken stock should have decent body and a mild, savoury flavour that enhances, rather than competes with, the sauces, casseroles and soup bases you make with it. This version is a good basic stock – arguably the most versatile type of stock. Ideally it should have full, clean flavours of chicken and aromatic vegetables and have more body than water. If it gels at least slightly when chilled, that's a good sign as far as body is concerned. If you have a slow cooker, cook on low overnight to make the best stock you've ever tasted (otherwise known as bone broth).

If you're using a raw chicken carcass, preheat the oven to 220°C (425°F/gas mark 7) and roast the carcass in a tin for about 40 minutes, until golden. This helps to draw out the flavour and caramelises the bones. Drain through a colander to get rid of any excess fat, then chop up the carcass.

Place the chopped-up chicken carcass in a large pan and cover with 1.8 litres (3¼ pints) of cold water. Bring to the boil, then skim off any fat and scum from the surface. Reduce the heat to a simmer and tip in all the remaining ingredients.

Simmer gently for another 1½ hours, skimming occasionally and topping up with water if necessary. If you simmer it too vigorously it will become cloudy. Taste regularly to check the flavour. When you're happy with it, remove the pan from the heat and pass the stock through a sieve into a large bowl. Leave to cool and remove any fat that settles on the top, then store in the fridge in a plastic jug with a lid and use as required. →

NEVEN'S TOP TIP

This stock freezes well, so I always have some to hand. I normally make it when we've had a roast chicken for dinner. This stock can be stored in the fridge for up to three days or you can freeze it in 600ml (1 pint) cartons and defrost it when you need it.

VEGETABLE STOCK
MAKES 1.2 LITRES (2 PINTS)

2 leeks, trimmed and finely chopped

2 onions, finely chopped

2 carrots, cut into 1cm (½in) dice

2 celery sticks, finely chopped

1 fennel bulb, cut into 1cm (½in) dice

1 garlic bulb, cut in half crossways

100ml (3½fl oz) dry white wine

1 sprig of fresh thyme

1 bay leaf

1 star anise

1 tsp pink peppercorns

1 tsp coriander seeds

a pinch of salt

This is a great vegetable stock, as the flavour is wonderfully intense from the addition of the aromatic spices. I don't remove the skins of the onions so that I end up with a much darker, nicer colour. Using a homemade vegetable stock in your soups and stews will add a depth of flavour and goodness that can't be matched by a stock cube.

Place all the ingredients in a large pan and cover with 1.7 litres (3 pints) of cold water. Cover with a lid and bring to a simmer, then remove the lid and cook for another 45 minutes, until the vegetables are tender.

Either set aside for two days in the fridge to let the flavours marry together, or if you're short on time, strain through a fine-mesh sieve. Taste – if you find the flavour isn't full enough, return the stock to the pan and reduce until you're happy with it.

Leave to cool completely, then transfer to a plastic jug with a lid and store in the fridge until needed. Use as required.

NEVEN'S TOP TIP

If time allows, I like to leave this vegetable stock with all the vegetables and aromatics still in it for two days in the fridge so that the flavours can really infuse and develop. This gives a much fuller taste and is definitely worth the extra wait. Strain before use, then either use within 24 hours or you can freeze it in 600ml (1 pint) cartons and defrost it when you need it, so there is no reason not to always have some on hand.

1

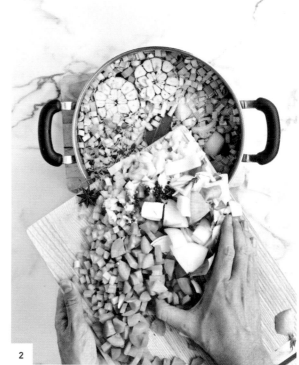

2

3

4

Pasta, Pizza, Pastry and Rice

PASTA

Pasta is a staple in most kitchens and many households eat it a couple times a week. The way pasta is cooked also affects its healthiness. These tips will steer you in the right direction to making perfect pasta. If you're serving the pasta with a sauce, I recommend draining the pasta about 3 minutes before the end of the cooking time stated on the packet instructions, then add it to the sauce and let it finish cooking in the sauce to soak up some of the flavours.

When cooking pasta, always use a large pan, as this is one time where size really matters. As a rough guide, 500g (18oz) of pasta should be cooked in a 6-litre (10½-pint) pan so that it has enough room to expand while cooking. If you don't cook the pasta in plenty of water, then it will get mushy and sticky.

Fill the pan two-thirds full of water and add 1 teaspoon of table salt per litre. If you're using sea salt, add a bit more. This might seem like a lot of salt, but the pasta will only take in a little as it cooks and the rest is drained away. It's worth remembering that pasta is essentially just flour, eggs and water, so it needs the salt for flavour. Many chefs say that you need to salt the water until it tastes like the sea.

Make sure the water is boiled, which means the water is moving around the pan with big bubbles. The initial plunge into the boiling water is critical to the texture of the final pasta and it also helps you to time the pasta better.

Once I have tipped the pasta into the boiling water I always give it a stir, otherwise I find that the pasta sticks together and cooks unevenly. Put a lid on so that the water comes back to a rolling boil quickly, then remove the lid.

As for cooking time, I always follow the timings on the box or packet, but this is only a guide. For the healthiest and tastiest way to cook pasta, you want to cook it just until it's al dente, which means 'to the tooth' or 'to the bite'. If overcooked, the glycaemic index will rise, whereas pasta that is cooked just until it's al dente is digested and absorbed slower than overcooked, mushy pasta. The best timer is your mouth, so start tasting the pasta at 20-second intervals starting from a minute or two before you think the pasta might be ready.

Don't drain all the pasta water away, as a teacup full of water can make a great addition to your sauce before adding the pasta. The salty, starchy water not only adds flavour, but it also helps to combine the pasta and sauce together and will help to thicken the sauce.

The way you drain the pasta can also affect the flavour and texture. If cooking long pasta such as spaghetti, try using tongs to transfer the pasta from the water to the sauce. For all short pasta shapes, drain it in a colander in the sink. Just make sure you don't let it sit too long or it will stick together. Finally, don't be tempted to rinse cooked pasta or you will rinse away the starch, which not only contributes to the flavour but also helps the sauce to adhere to it.

There you have it – perfectly cooked pasta that can be tossed with nothing more than a drizzle of extra virgin olive oil or a knob of butter. $\rightarrow$

Never add oil to your pasta cooking water – it does more harm than good. Since oil is less dense than water, it creates a layer across the top of the water. When the pasta is drained it's poured through this oily layer, which leaves a fresh coat of oil on the pasta, which in turn prevents it from soaking up any sauce as quickly as it should.

1

2

3

4

LASAGNE
SERVES 6

6–9 dried egg lasagne sheets (see the tip on the next page)

900ml (1½ pints) ragù sauce (page 179)

900ml (1½ pints) béchamel sauce (page 189)

50g (2oz) Parmesan cheese, freshly grated

TO SERVE

salad (page 20)

garlic bread

Lasagne is the perfect dish to feed a crowd and everyone seems to love it, young or old. I like to make mine the day before I want to eat it and then leave it in the fridge overnight covered with cling film. I find that this gives the lasagne sheets time to absorb the meaty ragù sauce so that it cuts much better the following day once it has been baked in the oven.

Preheat the oven to 180°C (350°F/gas mark 4).

Line a 2.75-litre (5-pint) ovenproof dish that is 5cm (2in) deep with two to three lasagne sheets, breaking them up to fit as necessary. Add half of the ragù sauce and spread it into an even layer. Spread over a third of the béchamel sauce. Cover with another layer of lasagne sheets. Use the rest of the ragù sauce to make another layer, then pour over another third of the béchamel sauce. Cover with the remaining lasagne sheets and spread the rest of the béchamel sauce on top, then scatter over the Parmesan.

Bake in the oven for 45–60 minutes, until the lasagne is bubbling and lightly golden. The exact cooking time depends on whether it's fridge cold. At this point the lasagne can be kept in the fridge for two days or frozen, covered with cling film, then reheated in the oven for 1 hour. Either way, allow to rest for 20 minutes, as it tastes better warm than piping hot.

Divide into sections with a fish slice and transfer to warmed serving plates. Add some salad to the side and serve with a basket of garlic bread. →

NEVEN'S TOP TIP

Look out for Italian bronze die egg lasagne sheets in the Dunnes Stores Simply Better range. They are made by La Campofilone in a village by the same name in a very traditional way. Their pasta is extra thin and almost melts in your mouth. The dried free-range egg pasta has a richer flavour with a more porous texture and is a better match for the ragù and béchamel sauce. As the lasagne sheets are the dish's most important ingredient, it would be a shame to let the pasta fade into the background.

1

4

5

Meals

CHICKEN KORMA
SERVES 4–6

12 skinless, boneless chicken thighs

250ml (9fl oz) natural yogurt or coconut milk (Thai Gold is best)

4 tbsp sunflower oil

1 cinnamon stick

10 cardamom pods, lightly crushed

1 onion, finely chopped

4 garlic cloves, grated

2.5cm (1in) piece of fresh root ginger, peeled and grated

50g (2oz) ground almonds

2 tsp ground cumin

2 tsp ground coriander

¼ tsp chilli powder

1 tsp tomato purée

4 tbsp cream

2 tsp garam masala

1 tsp saffron strands, soaked in a little water

sea salt and freshly ground black pepper

TO SERVE

fresh coriander leaves, to garnish

fluffy basmati rice (see page 65)

lime wedges

This is a delicious curry with a milder, creamier taste than other curries, which makes it a great one for all the family to enjoy. To make it into more of a celebration meal that will rival any takeaway, add some packets of poppadoms or naan bread, a nice lemony green salad, a jar of mango chutney and some natural yogurt. Serve the adults ice-cold beers and you'll be guaranteed that everyone will have a great time!

Cut the chicken into large bite-sized chunks and marinate in half of the yogurt or coconut milk for at least 2 hours, but overnight in the fridge is prefect, to tenderise the meat. Take it out half an hour before you want to cook to allow it to come back to room temperature.

Heat a large heavy-based pan or casserole with a lid over a medium-high heat. Add the oil, then add the cinnamon stick and cardamom pods. Once the cardamom starts to pop, add the chicken and brown on all sides, in batches if necessary, then take it out of the pan with a tongs and set aside.

Reduce the heat and add the onion. Fry for several minutes, until softened and a medium-brown colour, stirring occasionally but not constantly or the onion will not have time to catch and caramelise a little.

Add the garlic, ginger and ground almonds and cook, stirring, for 3–4 minutes, until lightly browned. Tip in the cumin, coriander and chilli powder and cook, stirring, for 30 seconds. Stir in the tomato purée and cook for another minute.

Add the cream, garam masala and saffron with the rest of the yogurt or coconut milk, stirring until combined. Return the chicken pieces to the pan and stir to coat them in the spice paste. Season to taste. Bring to a simmer, then cover the pan and reduce the heat to very low. Simmer gently for 15–20 minutes, until the chicken is cooked through and tender. →

Put the chicken korma into a serving dish and garnish with the coriander. Serve with the basmati rice and lime wedges.

NEVEN'S TOP TIP

If you find the amount of different spices needed too daunting, then consider using a ready-made curry paste. There are plenty available, from small artisan Irish companies to supermarket own label. As a general rule, use about 2 heaped tablespoons instead of all of the spices listed and you can also omit the tomato purée.

CURRY VARIATIONS

Thigh meat is cheaper and tastier than breast meat, but you can use breast if you prefer – it just takes less time to cook and is a little harder to keep moist. This curry would also be delicious with prawns or firm white fish. There is no need to cook them off at the beginning – simply add to the sauce and simmer gently for about 10 minutes, until tender. However, you could also use stewing beef or lamb and increase the cooking time to about 2½ hours.

VEGGIE CURRY (PERFECT FOR MEATLESS MONDAYS!)

Feel free to experiment with your favourite combinations of vegetables, such as courgette and sweet potato or butternut squash, aubergines and potatoes. Just remember that bigger, chunkier vegetables need longer cooking times, so add them at the start, whereas delicate vegetables like peas and spinach only need a few minutes, so they can go in right at the end.

1

4

THE STEW FORMULA
SERVES 4–6

3 tbsp rapeseed oil

2 onions, chopped

2 carrots, chopped

2 celery sticks, sliced

3 bay leaves

2 tbsp plain flour

300ml (½ pint) chicken or beef stock (from a cube is fine)

1 tbsp light muscovado sugar

2 tsp apple cider vinegar

sea salt and freshly ground black pepper

BEEF AND BEER (3 hours)

900g (2lb) diced stewing steak

1 heaped tbsp chopped fresh thyme

750ml (1 ¼ pints) beer (preferably an Irish craft beer)

PORK AND CIDER (2½ hours)

900g (2lb) diced stewing pork

1 heaped tbsp chopped fresh sage

750ml (1 ¼ pints) medium-dry cider

CHICKEN AND WHITE WINE (1½ hours)

900g (2lb) boneless, skinless chicken thighs, cut into 2cm (¾in) cubes

1 heaped tbsp chopped fresh tarragon

750ml (1¼ pints) dry white wine

LAMB AND RED WINE (2½ hours)

900g (2lb) diced stewing lamb

1 heaped tbsp chopped fresh rosemary

750ml (1¼ pints) red wine

TO SERVE

crusty bread or creamy mashed potatoes (page 155)

chopped fresh flat-leaf parsley, to garnish

steamed greens (page 163)

This is a great basic formula that works every time. Chunks of meat are cooked in liquid until they are meltingly tender, the flavour is deep and the liquid has developed into a thickened gravy. The meat should be cut into approximately 2cm (¾in) cubes and most prepared packs from the supermarket are this size. The way I've written this recipe allows you to easily chop and change it, using different meats, herbs and liquids, and in no time you'll be making up some of your own variations.

Preheat the oven to 160°C (325°F/gas mark 3).

Heat a heavy-based pan or casserole with a lid over a medium-high heat. Pat dry any excess liquid from the meat or chicken with kitchen paper. Add 2 tablespoons of rapeseed oil to the pan or casserole, then add the meat or chicken and brown it in batches, leaving plenty of room around each piece to ensure that they brown nicely and don't end up stewing. Set aside on a plate.

Add the remaining 1 tablespoon of oil to the pan, then add the onions, carrots, celery sticks, bay leaves and your chosen herb. Season with salt and pepper and cook gently for about 10 minutes, until the vegetables are just beginning to caramelise and soften. Sprinkle over the flour and cook for another minute or two, stirring. →

Gradually pour in the booze that you're using and then the stock, then add the sugar and vinegar. Return the meat or chicken to the pan or casserole and bring to a simmer. Cover with a lid, then transfer to the oven for the times shown on the previous page, removing the lid about halfway through to help the liquid to reduce and to concentrate the flavours.

To serve, put some mashed potatoes into each warmed wide-rimmed bowl and ladle over some of the stew scattered with the parsley or just serve with some crusty bread. Have a bowl of some steamed greens alongside so that everyone can help themselves.

NEVEN'S TOP TIP

A good stew with crusty bread or creamy mashed potatoes and some greens is a delicious family dinner or good enough for a dinner party, because once it's cooking away in the oven you're free to do other things. It also freezes well or can be kept in the fridge for up to three days, and in my opinion the flavour only improves over time.

WHAT MEAT TO BUY

You can buy your meat in packets from the supermarket, ready to go, but if you prefer to go to the butcher or decide to use the butcher counter in the supermarket, it's worth knowing what you're looking for. For the best results, you'll be looking for a tough cut that has some marbling with a decent amount of fat and connective tissue, which melt and gelatinise during the long, slow cooking process to help the tenderness. My favourite cut for a stew is from the shoulder, often referred to as chuck steak for beef, but lamb neck is also a good option. If you're trimming it down yourself, get an extra 225–450g (8oz–1lb) to allow for the trim.

1

HOMEMADE BEEF BURGERS
MAKES 4

1 red pepper

500g (18oz) minced beef (see the tip on the next page)

1 onion, finely chopped

1 egg, beaten

25g (1oz) fresh white breadcrumbs

1 tbsp freshly grated Parmesan cheese

1 tbsp sweet chilli sauce

1 tbsp chopped fresh flat-leaf parsley

1 tsp chopped fresh thyme

1 tsp Dijon mustard

2 tbsp olive oil

sea salt and freshly ground black pepper

TO SERVE

4 slices of Dubliner or Cheddar cheese

1 red onion, thinly sliced

4 brioche or blaa buns, split in half

2 ripe vine tomatoes, sliced

25g (1oz) rocket

4 tbsp mayonnaise

4 heaped tbsp tomato relish

These beef burgers would also be delicious served with a salad using the salad formula on page 20. If the sun is shining cook them on a barbie, otherwise a griddle pan also works fine.

Preheat the oven to 220°C (425°F/gas mark 7).

Place the red pepper on a baking sheet and roast in the oven for 20–25 minutes, until the skin is blackened and blistered and the flesh has softened. Once it's cool enough to handle, peel away the skin and discard it along with the stalks and seeds, then finely dice the flesh.

Place the diced red pepper in a bowl with the minced beef, onion, egg, breadcrumbs, Parmesan, sweet chilli sauce, herbs and mustard. Season to taste, then divide into four even-sized portions. Using slightly wetted hands, shape into patties that are about 2.5cm (1in) thick. Put the burgers on a plate, cover them with cling film and chill in the fridge for at least 15 minutes or up to 1 hour to allow the burgers to firm up.

Preheat the grill.

Heat the olive oil in a large frying pan or griddle pan. Add the burgers and cook for 4–5 minutes on each side for medium or give them another couple of minutes if you prefer your burgers more well done. Transfer to a warm plate and place a slice of cheese on top of each one, then leave to rest.

Add the red onion to the frying pan and sauté for 5 minutes, until softened and lightly coloured around the edges. Arrange the split brioche or blaa buns on a grill rack and toast them under the grill. →

Arrange the bottoms of the toasted buns on warmed serving plates and cover with one or two tomato slices, then place a cheese-topped burger on each one. Scatter over the sautéed red onion, then add a small handful of rocket. Smear the tops of the toasted buns with the mayonnaise and place on top. Serve with a spoonful of tomato relish on the side.

NEVEN'S TOP TIP

What makes a good burger? You've got to start with the right minced beef, then you're well on your way to a tasty burger no matter what garnishes you decide to use. Choose one with a 20% fat content – if you're unsure, check with the butcher or someone on the meat counter in the super-market. Anything too lean won't be succulent enough. Try to get mince that has been made that day – you might be surprised to find out that all good butchers will do this every morning and throw out any mince that is not bought by closing time.

1

2

3

4

5

MEATBALLS
SERVES 4–8

225g (8oz) lean minced beef

225g (8oz) minced pork

25g (1oz) Parmesan cheese, freshly grated

8 cream crackers, crushed into crumbs

1 large egg, lightly beaten

1 tbsp chopped fresh flat-leaf parsley, plus extra to garnish

1 tbsp Dijon mustard

olive oil, for drizzling and cooking

sea salt and freshly ground black pepper

TO SERVE

600ml (1 pint) tomato sauce (page 177)

500g (18oz) spaghetti

These authentic Italian meatballs in a rich tomato sauce are delicious piled up on spaghetti, but the meatballs are so versatile. They are also just as good served in a rich meat gravy with mashed potatoes or try serving them American-style by stuffing leftover meatballs and tomato sauce into a roll.

Place the minced beef and pork in a bowl with the Parmesan, cream crackers, egg, parsley and Dijon mustard. Season with salt and pepper and use your hands to give everything a good mix. Shape into about 20 even-sized balls. Use a small ramekin, egg cup or ice cream scoop as a guide for the perfect size every time. Arrange on a flat baking sheet or tray that will fit in your fridge, drizzle over a little olive oil to lightly coat and chill for 1 hour if time allows.

Heat 1 tablespoon of olive oil in a deep-sided frying pan over a medium heat. Add the meatballs and cook for 8–10 minutes, until almost cooked through and nicely browned. Pour in the tomato sauce and simmer gently for another 10 minutes or so, until the sauce has slightly reduced and thickened.

Meanwhile, plunge the spaghetti into a large pan of boiling salted water and simmer for 8–10 minutes, until tender but still with a little bite, or as the Italians say, al dente. (For more detailed instructions on how to cook pasta, see page 57.) Drain well and return to the pan, then add a few ladlefuls of the tomato sauce to coat the pasta.

Divide the spaghetti between warmed pasta bowls, then spoon the meatballs and the rest of the tomato sauce on top. Scatter over some chopped fresh parsley to serve. →

You can flash freeze the meatballs if you want to use a few at a time. Place the raw meatballs on a baking tray spaced well apart and freeze solid before transferring to a ziplock bag. That way, you can use as many as you need. Arrange them on a baking sheet or tray to thaw out for a couple of hours at room temperature before cooking them off.

1

SHEPHERD'S PIE
SERVES 6-8

2 tbsp rapeseed oil

675g (1½lb) lean minced lamb

a knob of butter

2 onions, finely chopped

2 carrots, diced

3 celery sticks, diced

100g (4oz) button mushrooms, sliced

1 tsp chopped fresh thyme

½ tsp ground cinnamon

1 tbsp Worcestershire sauce

2 tsp tomato purée

2 tsp tomato ketchup

300ml (½ pint) white wine

25g (1oz) plain flour

300ml (½ pint) chicken or beef stock (from a cube is fine)

sea salt and freshly ground black pepper

FOR THE MASH

1kg (2¼lb) Rooster potatoes, peeled and cut into chunks

75g (3oz) mature Cheddar cheese, grated

50g (2oz) butter, plus a little extra

TO SERVE

buttered peas

This has to be the ultimate comfort food that should only need to be eaten with a fork, preferably in a wide shallow bowl. Imagine settling down on the sofa with this, a mug of tea and a slice of thickly buttered bread for mopping up – life can't get much better! It's great to have one of these stashed in your freezer to help you to feed a large group at short notice. If you want to cook it from frozen, simply cover with tin foil and bake in the oven for 1 hour, until bubbling and golden brown.

Put a frying pan over a high heat and add a little of the oil. Season the minced lamb, then add it to the pan to fry in batches. Don't cover the surface of the pan completely, as adding too much meat will reduce the temperature of the pan and the meat won't brown. Avoid over-stirring the mince as it fries. Leave it alone and allow it to develop a good brown colour before breaking it up with a wooden spoon and turning it over. Drain in a colander to remove any excess fat.

Wipe out the pan, then add the butter and allow it to melt over a medium heat. Add the vegetables and thyme and season with the cinnamon and some salt and pepper. Cook for 5–6 minutes, stirring occasionally, until the veg are starting to soften.

Tip in the browned lamb mince, stirring to combine, then stir in the Worcestershire sauce, tomato purée and ketchup. Pour in the wine and scrape up all the crusty brown bits stuck to the bottom of the pan, then allow the liquid to reduce by three-quarters.

Sprinkle over the flour and cook for 2–3 minutes, stirring. Gradually pour in the stock and bring to a gentle simmer. Cook for 1 hour, until meltingly tender. If the sauce becomes too thick, add a little more water. →

During the last half an hour of cooking time, make the mash. Put the potatoes in a pan of cold salted water. Cover and bring to the boil, then reduce the heat and simmer for 15–20 minutes, until tender. Drain the potatoes and return to the pan over a low heat for 2–3 minutes to remove as much moisture as possible. Remove the pan from the heat, then mash with a potato masher until smooth. Beat in the cheese and butter and season to taste.

Preheat the grill.

Spoon the mince into a baking dish, then spoon the mash on top. Dot with a little more butter and grill until golden. Alternatively, leave to cool completely and store in the fridge for up to two days, then preheat the oven to 180°C (350°F/gas mark 4) and cook on the bottom shelf for 45 minutes, until bubbling and brown. Serve straight to the table with a dish of buttered peas alongside.

1

NEVEN'S TOP TIP

To make this recipe into a cottage pie, replace the lamb with beef. There are now different types of mince available in supermarkets and most butchers. As a general rule, the higher the price, the better quality the meat and the lower the fat content. If you're lucky enough to have some leftover roast lamb or beef, it makes the best pie. Follow the instructions above but add the diced meat once the sauce has been made, as the meat has already been cooked, and use any leftover gravy instead of stock.

4

HOW TO CHOOSE THE RIGHT STEAK

Striploin: A perfect all-rounder. The most well-known steak, this prime cut is gently marbled and has a melt-in-the-mouth succulence. It's almost as tender as the fillet but with a more generous portion size that will satisfy the heartiest of appetites.

Rib-eye: The chef's favourite. This cut has an open-fibre texture and a marbling of creamy fat. Cook with the surrounding fat still attached, then remove it afterwards. The fat adds flavour and bastes the meat during the cooking process.

Fillet: The most expensive cut. It's very lean and, because it has short fibres, very tender. The best pieces come from the middle of the fillet, not the end. It's also important that the sinewy chain that runs down the side has been removed. Each fillet is carefully hand cut into the perfect portion for one.

Sirloin: Great for all the family. It has a good marbling of fat with a layer of creamy fat on one side – this should be left on for cooking, then removed if you like. It has a unique flavour with a stronger, more mature taste.

TO COOK THE STEAKS

Whatever steak you choose, remove it from the packaging and allow it to come back up to room temperature for at least 20 minutes before you cook it. As a rough guide, serve 175g (6oz) for adults and 100g (4oz) steaks for children, although most now come prepared from the supermarket anyway.

A heavy-duty frying pan with a thick base, ideally one with a non-stick coating, will achieve good results, as will a heavy griddle pan or cast iron frying pan. Heat over a moderate heat for fillet, hot for sirloin or striploin and very hot for rib-eye. Season with salt and pepper just before cooking the steak. Don't be tempted to season a steak until just before cooking, as salt draws moisture out from meat.

Add a swirl of olive oil to the pan, then add the steaks and cook for 1½–2½ minutes on each side for medium rare. Add a lightly crushed garlic clove and fresh thyme sprig for extra flavour, if liked.

The exact cooking time will depend on the thickness of the steaks and fillet steaks take a little less time – allow 1–2 minutes longer if you prefer your steaks more well done.

For fillet steak, you'll need to cook it around the edges too. Don't be tempted to pierce the steak while it's cooking or turn it too often – once is enough.

To check how well done your steak is, press the steak lightly with your fingertip – when rare it will feel soft, medium-rare will be slightly bouncy and well done will be much firmer.

Add a knob of butter to the pan and allow to foam a little, then baste the steaks. Transfer to a plate and rest for 5–10 minutes (see the tip on the next page). This allows the fibres of the meat to relax and reabsorb the free-running juices. Slice along the grain, cutting off any fat, then arrange on a warmed serving plate with some sautéed mushrooms and garnish with snipped fresh chives, if liked. Have chunky chips (page 147) on the side. →

Once cooked, a steak should rest at room temperature for
at least 5 minutes and ideally around half of the cooking
time – it will stay warm for up to 10 minutes loosely covered
in tin foil. Pure science comes into play here – the fibres of
the meat will reabsorb the free-running juices, resulting in
a moist and tender finish to your steak.

HOW TO COOK FISH

Well-cooked fish should have a delicate crust and still be moist and quivering. If it's cooked beyond that point it will seize up and start to harden, then go gritty. Fish is delicate and needs your full attention, but the good news is that it's only for a very short time. Many chefs start by searing the fish fillet on one side in a frying pan, then flipping and finishing the cooking in a hot oven. The result is a nicely seared fillet that is perfectly cooked.

Sear-roasting works well for many types of fish, such as salmon, cod, hake and haddock. Firm-fleshed fish work brilliantly with this technique, rather than fragile fillets like plaice and sole.

A heavy-duty ovenproof frying pan is vital to pulling off this technique, particularly to create the seared crust. It's also vital not to crowd the pan or the fillets will end up steaming instead of searing, so it's worth cooking in batches if necessary. First preheat the oven to 220°C (425°F/gas mark 7) and heat an ovenproof frying pan over a medium heat. Add a little oil, then add the seasoned 150g (5oz) fish fillets, presentation side down. Now leave them alone for 3–4 minutes, as moving them around will prevent the crust from forming. When you think it's ready, gently lift a corner with a fish slice to see if it's nicely browned. If it is, you're ready to flip the fillets and put them into the oven to finish cooking. Roast in the oven for another 5 minutes, until just tender and cooked through. To test if your fish is cooked, make a small cut with a small sharp knife to see if the flesh has turned from translucent to opaque.

Roasting the fish will not give you the same seared crust, but it will still be delicious and can leave you free to get the other parts of your meal ready. Add some lemon-flavoured rapeseed or olive oil or softened butter with a little crushed garlic, some seasoning and perhaps a little lemon rind and chopped fresh herbs for extra flavour. Put each 150g (5oz) firm fish fillet on a rectangle of parchment paper on a baking sheet and smear over the oil or butter mixture. Pop in the oven for 6–8 minutes, until just tender.

Pan-frying a fillet of plaice or sole takes less than 10 minutes from start to finish. Have flour, butter, lemon wedges and hot plates ready. Put a couple tablespoons of plain flour on a plate and season with salt and pepper, mixing it with your fingers. Turn each fish fillet in the flour to coat and shake off any excess. Heat a large frying pan over a medium heat. Add a couple tablespoons of butter. As soon as it foams, add the floured fish fillets, flesh side down. Cook for 2 minutes, then turn over and cook for another 2–3 minutes, depending on how thick the fillets are. Transfer to the hot plates and add a squeeze of lemon to serve.

Steaming fish is elegant in its simplicity. You will need a heatproof plate that fits into your steamer (or use a trivet that fits into your wok or a large pan). Otherwise, bamboo steamers are very reasonable if you pick them up from an Asian supermarket. Most fish can be steamed, although I think that sole, sea bass, hake, sea trout, plaice and scallops, which are possibly the nicest treat of all, work best cooked this way. First rinse the fish and dry well with kitchen paper. If you want to add some aromatics, place the fish on a bed of shredded spring onions, then sprinkle the fish lightly with a little soy sauce and perhaps a scattering of fresh ginger cut into the finest threads (julienne). Steam for 8–12 minutes, depending on how thick the fillets are. It's easy to check – just wiggle a knife in between the flakes and see if the fish is opaque all the way through. →

If you like a sauce with your fish, they don't come any simpler than this 1-minute wonder. Once you've cooked the fish, quickly wipe out the pan with kitchen paper to remove any burned bits. Return the pan to a medium heat, then add a good knob of butter and swirl it until it foams. Add a sprinkling of chopped fresh flat-leaf parsley and finish with a squirt of lemon. Drizzle over the fish to serve. Delicious with a few radishes and a wedge of lemon

1

2

3

4

5

SAVOURY PIE
SERVES 4–6

Once I've gone to the trouble of making a stew (see the stew formula on page 87) it's great to get two days out of it, so I often end up using the leftovers to make a pie. It completely changes the flavours and there will be no complaints about having the same dinner again! This works with any of the meat and chicken variations.

Preheat the oven to 180°C (350°F/gas mark 4). Fill a pie dish with 675g (1½lb) of cooled leftover stew. Take one quantity of shortcrust pastry (page 73) from the fridge. Dust the work surface and your rolling pin with flour, then roll out the pastry to the thickness of a €1 coin. Once it's large enough to cover the pie dish easily, gently wrap the pastry around the rolling pin and unroll it over the dish. Run a sharp knife around the edge of the dish to trim off any excess pastry, then brush the edge of the pie dish underneath with beaten egg. Using a fork, press down the edge of the pastry to crimp it and help to secure it to the dish. Shape the trimmings into leaves and use to decorate the top, if liked. Make a hole in the middle of the dough with the tip of the knife and brush with egg wash (beaten egg with a splash of milk). Bake in the oven for about 40 minutes, until the pastry is crisp and golden. Serve straight to the table. →

Savoury pie

FISH PIE
SERVES 4-6

This fish pie is perfect for a family celebration, as once all the prep is done you've literally got nothing to do but pop it into the oven. Lots of supermarkets are now selling packets of mixed seafood, which are perfect for using in fish pies. Keep a look out and if you buy one you want it to be 750g (1lb 10 oz) in weight.

3 eggs

2 large shallots

2 celery sticks

300ml (½ pint) milk

2 bay leaves

a few black peppercorns

250g (9oz) salmon fillet, skin on and pin bones removed

250g (9oz) firm white fish fillets (such as cod, haddock or hake), skin on and pin bones removed

200g (7oz) raw peeled king prawns

50g (2oz) butter

200g (7oz) baby spinach

40g (1½oz) plain flour

150ml (¼ pint) cream

2 tbsp chopped fresh flat-leaf parsley

sea salt and freshly ground white pepper

FOR THE POTATO TOPPING

675g (1½lb) Rooster potatoes, peeled and cut into chunks

75g (3oz) mature Cheddar cheese, grated

25g (1oz) butter

TO SERVE

buttered peas

Preheat the oven to 180°C (350°F/gas mark 4).

To make the topping, put the potatoes in a pan of cold salted water. Cover and bring to the boil, then reduce the heat and simmer for 15–20 minutes, until tender. Drain the potatoes and return to the pan over a low heat for 2–3 minutes to remove as much moisture as possible. Remove the pan from the heat, then mash with a potato masher until smooth. Beat in the cheese and butter and season to taste.

Meanwhile, place the eggs in a pan with enough cold water to cover. Bring to the boil, then reduce the heat to a simmer and cook for 10–12 minutes, until hard-boiled. Drain under cold running water, then crack against the sink to break the shells. Remove the shells and cut the eggs into quarters.

Roughly chop one of the shallots and one of the celery sticks and place in a wide pan with the milk, bay leaves and peppercorns. Add the fish fillets, then bring to a simmer and cook for 3 minutes, until the fish is just tender. Stir in the prawns for the last 30 seconds of the cooking time. Transfer to a plate, then roughly flake, discarding the skin and bones. Strain the milk into a jug, discarding the vegetables, bay leaves and peppercorns.

Heat a knob of the butter in a pan. Add fistfuls of the spinach, adding another handful as the previous one wilts down. Cook for 1 minute, then tip into a colander to drain. →

Add the rest of the butter to the pan. Finely chop the remaining shallot and celery and add to the pan, stirring to coat. Sauté for 3–4 minutes, then add the flour and stir over a low heat for 1 minute. Gradually add the reserved milk, beating until smooth. Simmer for 2–3 minutes, until nicely thickened. Season to taste, then stir in the cream and allow to thicken and reduce down a little before stirring in the parsley.

Layer up the flaked fish, prawns and hard-boiled eggs in an ovenproof dish with small mounds of the spinach and spoonfuls of the sauce. Spread the mashed potatoes on top and bake in the oven for 25–30 minutes, until bubbling and golden.

Serve the fish pie straight to the table with a separate bowl of buttered peas.

NEVEN'S TOP TIP

For a change, try adding some smoked fish to this pie, such as smoked haddock or hot smoked salmon. The smoky flavour is a lovely addition and just a small amount of smoked fish will flavour the whole dish – I'd say no more than 100g (4oz) is about right.

1

4

GLAZED HAM
SERVES 6–8

1 x 1.75kg (3lb 14oz) gammon joint

1 onion, roughly chopped

1 carrot, roughly chopped

1 celery stick, roughly chopped

2 bay leaves

1 tsp black peppercorns

500ml (18fl oz) dry cider

1 tbsp Dijon mustard

2 tbsp Demerara or light muscovado sugar

I like cooking this on a Sunday instead of a roast and having the leftovers for lunchboxes during the week. It's also very handy to have in the summer when you're looking for a speedy supper or as part of a picnic served with a freshly cooked new potato salad or omelette. The ham is effectively cooked before going into the oven so baking it is not strictly necessary, although for me the rich, dark, spicy, sweet glaze is absolutely the best bit. Either way, the cooked ham will keep for up to a week covered with cling film in the fridge or you can slice and store it in the freezer in handy bags for up to two months.

Soak the gammon in cold water overnight to remove any excess saltiness, then rinse well and place in a large pan with a lid. Cover with fresh cold water. Add the onion, carrot, celery, bay leaves and peppercorns. Slowly bring to the boil, then cover and simmer very gently for 1 hour 30 minutes, until just cooked through and tender, periodically skimming off and discarding any white froth that comes to the surface. Remove from the heat and leave to cool in its liquid for 30–40 minutes.

Preheat the oven to 200°C (400°F/gas mark 6).

Remove the gammon joint from the cooking liquid and carefully cut away the rind and some of the excess fat. Lightly slash the remaining fat and place the ham in a small roasting tin. Pour in the cider, then smear the ham with the mustard and sprinkle over a thick layer of the sugar.

Bake in the oven for 25–30 minutes, until sticky and caramelised. Remove from the oven and leave to rest in a warm place for at least 20 minutes before carving what you need. Leave to cool completely and put on a plate, then cover well with cling film and keep in the fridge to use as required. →

I often add a couple of star anise to the water with the rest of the aromatics. It gives the ham a wonderful fragrant flavour, particularly when it's served cold.

3

4

CARBONARA
SERVES 4

500g (18oz) dried egg spaghetti

2 tbsp olive oil

2 garlic cloves, sliced

175g (6oz) slab of pancetta or dry-cured bacon, diced (see the tip on the next page)

4 eggs

2 egg yolks

100g (4oz) Parmesan cheese, freshly grated

fresh nutmeg, to serve

sea salt and freshly ground black pepper

This classic Italian pasta dish has its origins in or near Rome. In my opinion it should always be made with spaghetti so that the rich sauce clings to the pasta, allowing you to almost slurp it up when you're eating it. The ratio should be 3 to 1 in favour of the spaghetti. I tried and tested many different versions of the sauce for this book and decided that the use of cream isn't necessary. I found that it dilutes the delicate flavour of the eggs and Parmesan, plus it makes the sauce looser, preventing it from clinging to the spaghetti. This may be a simple dish but the devil is in the detail, so carefully follow the instructions on how to add the eggs to a hot pan so that you don't end up with scrambled egg pasta!

Cook the spaghetti in a large pan of boiling salted water until al dente (for further instructions on how to cook pasta perfectly, see page 57).

Meanwhile, heat the oil in a separate large pan over a low heat. Add the garlic and cook for a few minutes, until golden brown, then remove the garlic with a wooden spoon. This will give your oil a lovely subtle garlic flavour but won't ruin the smoothness of the sauce.

Add the pancetta or bacon to the flavoured oil, raise the heat to medium and sauté for 2–3 minutes, until it's golden and translucent but not brown around the edges.

Beat the eggs and egg yolks in a bowl, then stir in most of the Parmesan, reserving the rest for garnish. Season with pepper.

Scoop out a small mug of the pasta cooking water, then drain the spaghetti well. Tip it into the pan with the pancetta and toss to coat.

Remove the pan from the heat and tip in the egg mixture, tossing the pasta quickly with a tongs. Once it has begun to thicken, add a splash of the cooking water to loosen the sauce a little. Toss again and divide between warmed serving bowls. Add a light grating of nutmeg to each one, then garnish with the reserved Parmesan to serve.

NEVEN'S TOP TIP

Italians always make this with pancetta, which is dry-cured, normally unsmoked and is usually from a slab rather than from prepared slices or diced. Look out for slabs of dry-cured streaky bacon in your local farmers market and cut it into cubes yourself. These would also freeze well, so you could have portions of it ready to use for the days you're under pressure to get a dinner on the table fast.

1

The Roast

HOW TO MAKE A ROAST DINNER, STEP BY STEP

A properly cooked roast dinner is a joy and loved by everyone, including fussy children, awkward teenagers and critical relatives who can be hard to please! Traditionally a roast dinner was always cooked on a Sunday. In my parents' lifetime this was because it was expensive and looked forward to as a treat when there was more relaxed family time.

If there are people around, delegate jobs – get someone to lay the table and another to take care of the drinks. Children often enjoy going out into the garden to find a few little flowers to brighten up the table.

This leaves you time to concentrate on the task in hand. It's important to learn how to pull it all together so that you absolutely nail it: juicy meat with crispy roast potatoes, perfect gravy and some colourful vegetables. What better way to feed a large group of family or friends?

The best way to approach it is to decide what time you would like to serve and work backwards from that, making a quick note of a time plan.

Take the meat or chicken out of the fridge about 1 hour before you plan to cook it. Arrange the oven shelves so that everything you want to cook will fit. This is particularly relevant if you want to cook everything in one oven.

Preheat the oven and prepare the joint as described in the recipe. Prepare the roast potatoes so that they go into the top shelf of the oven half an hour before the meat is going to come out.

Once your meat is cooked, take it out of the oven. Increase the oven temperature of the potatoes to 220°C (425°F/gas mark 7), give the potatoes a good toss and finish cooking them while the meat is resting and you make the gravy (page 193).

I always cook a nice crisp seasonal green vegetable, or if there's nothing exciting available, I'll serve frozen peas, which everyone always loves. I normally do baked root vegetables in a bag (see page 161) as their cooking time is very flexible, the technique is extremely forgiving and they always seem to stay wonderfully moist and succulent. Most importantly, they stay piping hot until I open their foil bag before putting them on hot serving plates, which are also crucial. There's nothing worse than a cold roast dinner because you've forgotten to heat the plates! I also always heat the gravy jug so that the gravy is piping hot when it goes onto the table.

NEVEN'S TOP TIP –
HOW TO PULL IT ALL TOGETHER AT A GLANCE

- Remove the cooked meat to rest and increase the oven temperature of the potatoes.
- Heat the gravy jug and serving plates, not forgetting an extra one to carve the meat onto.
- Make the gravy and keep it warm.
- Once the meat has rested, carve onto the warmed plate and then arrange on warmed serving plates.
- Put the green vegetable on to steam or cook.
- Open the foil packaging of the baked root vegetables (page 161) and then arrange on the plates.
- Drain the green vegetable and toss in a knob of butter. Put on the plates with the crispy roast potatoes.
- Arrange the plates on the table.
- Pour the gravy into the heated gravy jug and put straight onto the table to serve.
- Sit down and enjoy the fruits of your labour!

ROAST CHICKEN
SERVES 4

1 x 1.5kg (3¼lb) whole chicken, preferably free-range or organic (see the tip on the next page)

2 onions, peeled and halved

6 small carrots, peeled and cut in half lenghtways

2 celery sticks, trimmed and cut into quarters

1 lemon, halved

1 small bunch of fresh thyme

50g (2oz) butter, softened

about 200ml (7fl oz) white wine or water

sea salt and freshly ground black pepper

If you are a complete novice when it comes to cooking, then roasting a chicken is a great dinner to master. The holy grail is crispy skin and juicy meat. If you don't want to pierce the thigh to check that it is cooked, try tugging at a drumstick – it should feel loose and easy to move.

Remove the chicken from the fridge 1 hour before you plan to cook it and discard any packaging.

Preheat the oven to 190°C (375°F/gas mark 5). Get a shelf ready in the middle of the oven.

Scatter the vegetables over the base of a roasting tin that fits the chicken snugly but doesn't swamp it. Dry the chicken well with kitchen paper inside and out. Season the cavity liberally with salt and pepper, then stuff with the lemon halves and thyme.

Sit the chicken on the vegetables and spread the breast and legs all over with the butter, then season the outside with salt and pepper. Add a splash of the wine or water to help keep the vegetables moist. Tie the legs securely with butcher's string.

Place the chicken in the oven and leave undisturbed for 1 hour 20 minutes, until the chicken is cooked through and golden brown. Baste the chicken halfway through. If you think that the vegetables look a little dry, add another splash of wine or water to the tin to stop them from burning. To check that the chicken is fully cooked, pierce the thigh with a skewer – the juices should run clear.

Remove the cooked chicken from the oven and transfer to a warm plate, then leave to rest in a warm place covered with a layer of tin foil and a clean tea towel for at least 20 minutes before carving. Use the vegetables in the tin to make the gravy (see the recipe on page 193). →

To carve the chicken, carefully cut down between the leg and the breast, cutting through the joint so that the legs can be pulled away easily. Then cut between the thigh and drumstick. Place on a warmed plate. Angle the knife along the breastbone and carve off one side, then the other. The rest of the meat can be pulled off once the chicken is cold and used for another meal or in a sandwich.

Arrange on warmed plates with gravy, crispy roast potatoes (page 151) and your favourite vegetables.

NEVEN'S TOP TIP

If you can afford it, buy a free-range or organic chicken, as the flavour is always so much better. It also means that you're much more likely to get a second dinner out of the leftovers and even a third if you fancy making stock (see page 50) and using it to make a nice wholesome soup.

1

2

3

ROAST SIRLOIN OF BEEF
SERVES 4–6

Although I love a roast rib on the bone, this cut of beef is certainly the most popular joint available. I can understand why, as sirloin has a great flavour with a decent marbling of fat. It's also extremely easy to carve – I normally use a carving fork to help me hold it steady.

1kg (2¼lb) sirloin of beef

2 onions, cut into thick slices

2 carrots, thickly sliced on the diagonal

2 celery sticks, thickly sliced on the diagonal

1 bulb of garlic, halved

1 small bunch of fresh thyme and/or sage

rapeseed or olive oil, for cooking

about 300ml (½ pint) red or white wine or water

sea salt and freshly ground black pepper

TO SERVE

chopped fresh flat-leaf parsley, to garnish

creamed horseradish or mild mustard

Remove the joint from the fridge 1 hour before you plan to cook it and discard any packaging.

Preheat the oven to 220°C (425°F/gas mark 7).

Tip the vegetables, garlic and herbs into a roasting tin and season with salt and pepper, then drizzle over a little oil. Rub some more oil over the beef and season all over, then sit that in the middle of the vegetables. Add a splash of wine or water to the tin to prevent the vegetables from drying out.

Roast in the oven for 25 minutes, then reduce the heat to 180°C (350°F/gas mark 4) and add another splash of wine or water if you think the vegetables need it. Roast for another 1 hour for rare and 1½ hours for medium rare. Transfer the beef to a warm plate and leave to rest for at least 20 minutes, covered with tin foil and a clean tea towel. Use the vegetables left in the tin to make the gravy (see the recipe on page 193). Garnish with parsley.

Carve the beef sirloin into slices and arrange on warmed plates with gravy, crispy roast potatoes (page 151) and vegetables of your choice. Serve with creamed horseradish or mild mustard on the side. →

ROAST LEG OF LAMB
SERVES 6–8

1 x 2.25kg (5lb) leg of lamb

2 onions, sliced

2 carrots, sliced on the diagonal

2 celery sticks, sliced on the diagonal

1 bulb of garlic, separated into cloves but not peeled

1 small bunch of fresh rosemary and/or thyme, plus extra to garnish

200ml (7fl oz) white wine or water

extra virgin rapeseed or olive oil, for cooking

sea salt and freshly ground black pepper

TO SERVE

redcurrant jelly and/or mint sauce (optional – see the tip on the next page for mint sauce)

This is my favourite way of cooking lamb – simply roasted with lots of basting to keep it juicy and succulent, then incorporating all the meat juices and crusty bits into a perfect gravy (page 193) and homemade mint sauce (see the tip on the next page).

Take your lamb out of the fridge 1 hour before it goes into the oven. Remove all the packaging and dry well with kitchen paper.

Preheat the oven to 200°C (400°F/gas mark 6).

Pile the vegetables, garlic and herbs into the middle of a large roasting tin and drizzle with oil, then season with salt and pepper. Drizzle the lamb with oil and season with salt and pepper, then rub all over the joint.

Place the lamb on top of the vegetables and add the wine or water. Roast for 1 hour 30 minutes for rare, pink, blushing meat, basting the lamb at least three times during cooking, as this will help to keep it juicy and succulent.

To check that the lamb is cooked as you like it, insert a skewer into the centre, remove it, then press the flat of the skewer against the meat: as the juice runs out, you will see to what degree it is cooked – the pinker the juice, the rarer the meat. When it is cooked as you like it, transfer it to a carving board and cover loosely with a layer of tin foil and a clean tea towel. Keep it in a warm place to rest for 30 minutes while you make your gravy with the vegetables in the tin (see the recipe on page 193).

To carve the lamb, wrap the tea towel around the bone so that you can get a good grip on it. Using a sharp carving knife, cut into thin slices away from you. When you get down to the bone, just rotate the leg and start carving again. →

Arrange on warmed serving plates with crispy roast potatoes (page 151), vegetables of your choice and some gravy. Have a separate dish of redcurrant jelly and/or mint sauce, if liked.

NEVEN'S TOP TIP – MINT SAUCE

Once you know the trick, this delicious homemade mint sauce that is perfect with roast lamb literally takes only minutes to prepare. Strip the leaves from a 15g (½oz) bunch of fresh mint sprigs and put them in a jug with 1 tablespoon of caster sugar and 4 tablespoons of just-boiled water. Stir to dissolve the sugar and leave to cool. Stir in 4 tablespoons of white wine vinegar to serve.

The

Humble

Potato

HOMEMADE CHIPS
SERVES 4

4 large Rooster potatoes (about 1.5kg/3¼lb), peeled

1.2 litres (2 pints) vegetable oil, for deep-frying

a good pinch of flaky sea salt

Homemade chips should be perfectly crisp on the outside and super fluffy on the inside. At home we don't cook chips very often, so when we do make them, we definitely want the real deal. The secret is to cook them twice at two different temperatures, so you will need a deep-fat fryer or deep pan and a thermometer for this recipe.

Trim the potatoes into rectangles, then cut into 1cm (½in) slices, then cut again to make chips that are 1cm (½in) wide. Rinse the chips in plenty of cold water to remove the excess starch. If time allows, leave them to sit in a bowl of cold water for a couple of hours or even overnight.

If you're using a deep-fat fryer, heat the vegetable oil to 95°C (200°F). Alternatively, fill a deep, heavy-based pan one-third full with oil and use a sugar thermometer to check that it has reached the correct temperature. Otherwise you can test that the oil is hot enough with a sprig of fresh parsley – when it crackles but doesn't burn, the oil is ready. Take great care if using a pan: always watch over it and never fill it more than a third, as hot fat may bubble up when the potatoes are added.

Drain the chips and dry them really well on kitchen paper, then carefully lower them into the heated oil and cook for 10 minutes. This blanches them and ensures that they are completely cooked through without colouring them. Check that the chips are tender using the point of a knife, then remove from the oil using a slotted spoon or spider (as shown in the photos on page 149) if using a pan and drain on kitchen paper.

Increase the heat of the oil in the fryer or pan to 190°C (375°F). Lower in the blanched chips and cook for another 2–3 minutes, until crisp and golden brown. Shake off any excess fat, then quickly drain on kitchen paper and sprinkle with a little salt to serve. ->

Once the chips have been blanched so that they're cooked through and tender without any colour, they can be left to cool on a baking sheet lined with greaseproof paper. If you want to keep them for longer than an hour, cover them with cling film and chill in the fridge for up to 6 hours before cooking them – any longer and the potatoes are in danger of discolouring slightly.

3

4

CRISPY ROAST POTATOES
SERVES 4–6

1.5kg (3¼lb) potatoes, peeled and cut into even-sized pieces

sea salt

about 100ml (3½fl oz) rapeseed, olive or vegetable oil, beef dripping (James Whelan is a great brand) or duck or goose fat

When it comes to roast potatoes, I'm looking for really crunchy outsides and fluffy middles and this is the best method I have found for guaranteed results. If you're cooking a roast then it's fine to cook the potatoes on the top shelf of the oven at whatever temperature you need, but once the roast has been taken out to rest, increase the oven temperature to 220°C (425°F/gas mark 7) and roast the potatoes for another 30 minutes or so. Roast potatoes should be the last things to go on the plate just before serving.

Preheat the oven to 220°C (425°F/gas mark 7).

Place the potatoes in a pan of cold water with a pinch of salt, then cover and bring to the boil. Reduce the heat and simmer for 10 minutes – longer if you want a really crispy potato; sometimes I boil them until they have virtually collapsed. This is an important step, as it makes the potatoes crisper and they seem to better accept the flavour of the cooking fat and whatever additional flavourings you want to add.

Drain the parboiled potatoes and leave in the colander to cool slightly, then drag a fork all over them to make ridges in the flesh. Alternatively, give them a good shake in the colander to fluff up the edges.

Put a roasting tin in the oven with a 1cm (½in) depth of oil, dripping, or duck or goose fat for a few minutes, until just smoking. Carefully tip the potatoes into the hot oil, then quickly spoon the oil over the tops of the potatoes and season with salt. Always put the potatoes into hot fat – they will absorb less fat and crisp up much better. If you coat the potatoes in fat now, there is no need for basting.

Roast the potatoes in the oven for 35–45 minutes, turning twice to ensure they cook evenly, then carefully pour off most of the fat. Return the tin to the oven and cook for another 5 minutes, until crisp and golden. Serve immediately, as they don't like to hang around!

As regards what to cook roast potatoes in, all fats freeze very well, so do make the effort if you've got some left over from a roast – it really does make a world of difference to the flavour of your roast potatoes. I often add a couple sprigs of fresh herbs, such as rosemary or thyme, for extra flavour or a handful of unpeeled garlic cloves and/or the pared rind of a lemon.

1

2   3

MASHED POTATOES
SERVES 4–6

1.5kg (3¼lb) floury potatoes (preferably Roosters), peeled and cut into even-sized chunks

120ml (4fl oz) milk

75g (3oz) butter

sea salt and freshly ground black pepper

Once mastered, this recipe will ensure wonderfully smooth, creamy mashed potatoes every time. The fluffiest mash is made from floury, mealy potatoes, but I use Roosters, which seem to be able to give consistent results all year round. Should you need to keep the mash warm before serving, cover the surface with melted butter and the pan with foil, then whisk the butter into the mash just before serving.

Place the potatoes in a large pan of salted water. Bring to the boil, then reduce the heat, cover and simmer for 15–20 minutes, until the potatoes are tender without breaking up. Drain and return to the pan over a low heat to steam dry, then put a clean tea towel under the lid to soak up any excess moisture.

Mash the potatoes or pass them through a potato ricer or vegetable mouli if you want a really smooth finish. If you haven't got a ricer or mouli, don't worry – in that case, just mash the potatoes with a knob of the butter first, before you add any milk, so that you can really mash them hard to remove all the lumps without the mixture being too wet.

Heat the milk in a small pan or in the microwave. It's much easier to add hot liquid to the mashed potatoes rather than cold and the added bonus is that it helps to keep the mash nice and hot. Using a wooden spoon, beat in the butter until melted, then gradually beat in enough of the warm milk until you have a smooth, creamy mash. Alternatively, you can melt the butter with the milk in the saucepan, but the mash won't be quite as fluffy. The final beating is a vital part of creating a light mash. Season to taste with salt and pepper and serve at once. →

NEVEN'S TOP TIP

These mashed potatoes can be changed quite dramatically with a few additional ingredients depending on what you are serving them with. Enrich them with the addition of a couple tablespoons of cream or crème fraîche instead of the milk or try adding a spoonful of mild mustard or a sprinkling of fresh herbs – snipped fresh chives work particularly well. And let's not forget traditional champ, where thinly sliced spring onions are sautéed first in butter before being added, or colcannon, with the extra addition of cooked shredded kale or cabbage.

1

4

Vegetables

ROOT VEGETABLES

Root vegetables are the starchy tubers and taproots of plants. If we let them be they would provide the plant with the nourishment it needs to thrive. Instead, we pull them up and eat them and all their sweet, starchy flavour helps to fill us up. There are numerous ways to cook root vegetables, which include potatoes, sweet potatoes, carrots, turnips, swedes, parsnips, celeriac and beetroot.

Roasting brings out the sweetness in any root vegetable and their lightly charred exterior is delicious. Scrub the vegetables clean and peel unless they are the first crop of the season. Cut into even-sized pieces and toss with enough rapeseed or olive oil or melted butter (sometimes I use a mixture of oil and butter) to lightly coat them. Put in a roasting tin where they won't be too crowded and season with salt and pepper. They can also benefit from a sprinkling of chopped fresh herbs, such as thyme or rosemary, or even a hint of spice from cumin or chilli powder. Roast in a preheated oven (220°C/425°F/gas mark 7) for 30–40 minutes, until tender and lightly charred.

Steaming is an excellent option for the first crop of vegetables, particularly carrots, turnips, parsnips and new potatoes, or if you like the baby varieties. The flavour is delicate and sweet and there is absolutely no need to peel here – just rinse them under a cold running tap and cut off only the stalks, just a fraction above the end. This leaves the vegetable intact and preserves the natural flavour. Place them in a steamer, sprinkle with a little salt and steam for 5–7 minutes, until tender when pierced with a sharp knife but still retaining a little bite. Larger specimens also work with this method and you could use a mixture – just peel the vegetables first and cut into bite-sized pieces. Steam for 10–20 minutes, until tender, then mash with a knob of butter and season with plenty of black pepper to serve.

Baked root vegetables in a bag is possibly my favourite way of cooking this type of vegetable. I normally always do them for a Sunday roast, as they can be prepared in advance and just need to be popped in the oven about 1 hour before you need them. They will also keep warm for a reasonable amount of time in the unopened parcel, which can be helpful. Peel your chosen selection of root vegetables and cut them into even-sized batons. Place them in the middle of a large double sheet of tin foil, then scatter over a finely chopped shallot, a little chopped fresh thyme and a pinch of sugar and season with salt and pepper. Add 4 tablespoons of water and seal the parcel closed. Put on a baking sheet and roast in a preheated oven (180°C/350°F/gas mark 4) for 1 hour, until the vegetables are meltingly tender and slightly caramelised.

Root vegetable gratin is a great way to use root vegetables, as they all lend themselves perfectly to being peeled, thinly sliced, layered and baked until tender. Serve them as an elegant side dish or casual midweek supper with some crusty bread and perhaps a green salad. Note that if you want to add onions or leeks to a gratin you'll need to cook them first until softened. Layer up your vegetables of choice in a buttered baking dish and season with salt, pepper and a pinch of nutmeg as you go. Adding a good sprinkling of your favourite grated hard cheese also works well. Pour over enough vegetable stock (see the recipe on page 52) or cream to just barely cover the vegetables, or use half stock and half cream if you like. Sprinkle over a final layer of cheese or use breadcrumbs tossed in a little melted butter if you prefer. Bake in a preheated oven (190°C/375°F/gas mark 5) for 45–60 minutes, until completely tender when pierced with a sharp knife.

GREEN VEGETABLES

This section is designed to help you cook perfect green vegetables. All green veg need care and attention to get the best out of them. Trial and error teaches you when to recognise that they are cooked to perfection – after that point, they begin to deteriorate. If boiling green vegetables, the water should barely cover the vegetables as a brief encounter is really what you're looking for. Steaming is also a great option and in most cases steam rather than water helps to preserve more flavour. Another good option is to steam-fry, which is a traditional Chinese technique that cooks the veg at very high temperatures, which allows the little amount of water that you have added to evaporate quickly.

So which is the best method? There isn't one. All vegetables respond differently to different ways of cooking, so experiment to find out which ones you like best. Whatever way you decide to cook them, try to eat vegetables that are in season whenever possible. Not only will they taste better, but they should also be cheaper and have more nutrients as they should have had less travel time.

Boiling

Bring a pan of water to a rolling boil, then drop in the prepared vegetables. It's important that you don't try to cook too much at one time, as the water must return to the boil as soon as possible. Immediately put the lid on and simmer until done. The time will vary depending on the vegetable, but as a rough guide most will take 3–4 minutes, depending on their size. In the case of green beans, they should have a resistance when eaten, but no crunch. Lift the vegetables out of the water. If you are not going to serve them immediately, plunge them into a bowl of iced water. This is not essential to keep the colour, but if you leave them to cool at room temperature, the residual heat will continue cooking them. Reheat the vegetables in a mixture of butter and water, at a ratio of one-third butter to two-thirds water. Season with salt and pepper, then briefly drain to serve. To make cooked vegetables into a salad, add a couple finely chopped shallots to one quantity of salad dressing (see the recipe on page 197), then use this to season the vegetables instead of the butter emulsion.

Steaming

Cut the vegetables into even-sized pieces so that they will cook at the same time. You can mix the vegetables, but be aware that more tender vegetables like sugar snap peas or mangetout will cook faster then denser vegetables like broccoli florets. If you want to steam mixed vegetables at the same time, add the ones that take longer to cook first, then add the quicker-cooking ones after a few minutes. You can also cut the denser vegetables into slightly smaller pieces so that they cook more quickly and finish at the same time as the rest of the vegetables. Put your prepared vegetables into a steamer basket set over at least 2.5cm (1in) of simmering water. Check after 3 minutes unless you're cooking sugar snap peas and mangetout, which should be done in just 1 minute. Toss in a small knob of butter or lightly dress with a drizzle of your favourite extra virgin oil. Season with salt and pepper to serve. →

Steam-fry

Shred any leafy vegetables, discarding any tough stalks, or cut into bite-sized pieces. Heat 1 tablespoon of butter with 2 tablespoons of water and bring to a simmer over a high heat to form an emulsion. Tip in the vegetables with a pinch of salt and put on the lid. Shake vigorously and cook for 1½ minutes. Shake the pan again and cook for another 1½ minutes, then remove from the heat. Give everything a good stir and season with pepper before serving.

NEVEN'S TOP TIP

If cooking green beans, top and tail them, then soak in cold water for a couple of hours before using. Most beans have been picked long before they reach our supermarket shelves – a couple of months in some cases – so soaking them helps to rehydrate them.

1

2

3

SUMMER VEGETABLES

During the summer, many young vegetables don't even get cooked in our house, as to do so would just mask their flavour. I love making up salads with whatever we have plenty of in the garden, such as baby courgettes pared into ribbons and tossed into pasta or couscous with thinly sliced fennel, freshly podded peas and asparagus tips that have been halved again to make them easier to eat. Later on in the summer, though, I love barbecuing or oven roasting vegetables, the bonus being that they require very little attention.

Oven-roasted summer vegetables
Cut aubergines, courgettes and mixed coloured peppers into 2.5cm (1in) dice. Put into a roasting tin in a single layer and drizzle with rapeseed or olive oil, tossing to coat. Season with salt and pepper and roast in a preheated oven (220°C/425°F/gas mark 7) for 20 minutes. Remove from the oven and add some diced red onion, garlic and a scattering of torn fresh basil or thyme leaves, tossing to coat them evenly in the juices already in the tin. Roast in the oven for another 15 minutes, until the vegetables are lightly charred and tender. Serve hot or at room temperature with plenty of crusty bread to mop up all the delicious juices. These are great on their own, tossed with pasta, quinoa or couscous or served with barbecued meat or fish – the possibilities are endless!

Baby summer vegetables
To get the best colour and texture it's best to skin broad beans, so after shelling them, pour boiling water over them. Once the beans have cooled, simply slip off the outer skin and place in a bowl. Steam tiny baby carrots with trimmed spring onions and freshly podded peas for 3–4 minutes. Toss with the broad beans and put into a pan with a knob of butter or a dash of extra virgin olive oil. Add some chopped fresh mint and/or chives and heat gently for 1 minute, then season with salt and pepper to serve.

Roasted cherry tomatoes on the vine
These days our supermarkets stock cherry tomatoes on the vine all year round, but in the summer months, when they are at their most flavoursome, simply place the vines of cherry tomatoes in a roasting tin lined with parchment paper and drizzle over a little garlic- or chilli-infused rapeseed oil. Roast in a preheated oven (220°C/425°F/gas mark 7) for 8–10 minutes, until lightly charred and the skins are just beginning to burst. Serve with roasted fish or meat or even some bubbling goat's cheese for a simple quick supper. →

Roasted peppers

Char peppers until their skins are blackened and blistered in a hot oven or under the grill. This will take 30–40 minutes and the flesh should feel nice and tender when they are done. Place in a large bowl and cover with cling film to allow the skins to steam off. Remove all the skin, cores and seeds and slice up the flesh. Arrange on a plate and add a light drizzle of olive oil and a sprinkling of good balsamic vinegar. Season with salt and pepper and tear over a few fresh basil leaves to serve as a salad with some goat's cheese or as part of an antipasti platter with olives, Parma ham and buffalo mozzarella. They are also delicious with spicy sausage or barbecued meats.

NEVEN'S TOP TIP

The natural sweetness of vegetables begins to convert into starch from the moment that they are picked, so try to use up your vegetables when they are nice and fresh. The flavour really will be so much better and they will also contain more nutrients, so they are much better for you as well.

1   2   3

WINTER VEGETABLES

Besides the wonderful array of root vegetables that I have already covered on page 161, I also look forward to the other vegetables that winter has to offer: onions, young leeks, shallots, broccoli, Brussels sprouts, cauliflower, crisp varieties of cabbage and kale, celery and one of my all-time favourites, fennel.

Roast cabbage wedges

Cut the cabbage in half and remove the tough core, then cut into quarters. Arrange in a roasting tin with the cut sides up. Smear a little butter onto the cut sides and drizzle with oil. Season with salt and pepper and roast in a preheated oven (200°C/400°F/gas mark 6) for about 30 minutes, until tender when pierced with a sharp knife. Serve immediately.

Roast fennel wedges

Trim off the hard round stalks at the top of the fennel bulbs and discard the outer layers too. Cut the remainder into thin wedges and place in a large, shallow roasting tin. Drizzle over a little rapeseed oil and toss to coat, then season to taste. Place the fennel in the bottom shelf of a preheated oven (220°C/425°F/gas mark 7) and roast for 30–40 minutes, until the wedges have softened and are lightly browned, stirring once or twice to ensure even cooking. Serve with fish or as part of a salad.

Kale (curly kale, winter greens or sprout tops)

Always buy a generous quantity. It's always good value, which means you can be ruthless in cutting out tough, stringy stalks, keeping only the best leaves. Once they're prepped, put them on a chopping board with all the heads together at one end. Cut across if necessary to get them to all fit in the pan. Bring a pan filled with about 2cm (½in) of salted water to the boil. Once it's at a rolling boil, put in the stalk end of the greens, with the more delicate leaves on top so that they steam. Cover with a lid and leave to boil vigorously. After 5 minutes, test one of the tough stalks to make sure it's just cooked. Drain in a colander. If liked, you can toss the cooked greens in a pan with a knob of butter and a little diced onion and/or garlic. Serve immediately.

Creamed savoy cabbage

Heat a little rapeseed oil in a pan over a medium heat. Add 100g (4oz) each of finely diced carrot and celeriac and sweat gently for 3–4 minutes. Add 25g (1oz) of butter. Once it has melted, tip in 350g (12oz) of thinly sliced Savoy cabbage. Cook for 2–3 minutes, until the cabbage has wilted. Pour in 200ml (7fl oz) of cream, stirring to combine, and season to taste. Simmer to reduce and slightly thicken the cream. Serve immediately or keep for up to 12 hours covered tightly with cling film in the fridge.

Broccoli and cauliflower gratin

Put florets of steamed broccoli and cauliflower in a buttered baking dish and pour over enough cheese sauce (see the recipe on page 190) to coat. Scatter over a sprinkling of dried white breadcrumbs (panko) and some extra grated cheese and bake in a preheated oven (200°C/400°F/gas mark 6) for 25–30 minutes, until bubbling and golden. Serve straight to the table on its own or as a side dish with glazed ham (page 119) or roast chicken (page 129).

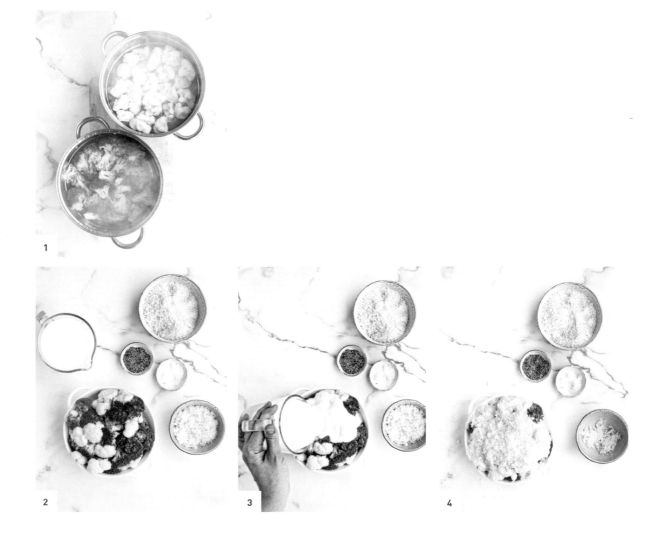

Sautéed brussels sprouts

Cook trimmed Brussels sprouts in boiling water or steam them for 5–6 minutes, until tender, then drain and refresh in cold water. Cut into halves or quarters depending on their size. Heat a good knob of butter in a large frying pan or wok and sauté the sprouts until lightly golden. Season with salt and pepper, then sprinkle over a little finely grated lemon rind and chopped fresh flat-leaf parsley, tossing to coat. Serve at once with chicken or ham.

Shallot compote

One very useful condiment to have in the fridge is a shallot compote, which could also be made with pearl onions. It's an excellent partner to beef or you can have it with sausages or a hunk of cheese and a few celery sticks with some bread for an instant late-night supper. Peel the shallots and put into a sauté pan in a single layer. Add 4 table-spoons of apple cider vinegar and a couple glasses of red wine. Bring to the boil, then reduce the heat to its lowest setting and cook very gently for about 1 hour, until the shallots are tender but still holding their shape. The resulting compote keeps well for weeks in a Kilner jar in the fridge and you'll find yourself using it again and again.

1 2 3

Sauces

TOMATO SAUCE
MAKES ABOUT 600ML (1 PINT)

1 x 400g (14oz) tin of Italian whole plum tomatoes (see the intro) or 6 large vine-ripened tomatoes

2 tbsp olive oil

1 onion, finely chopped

2 garlic cloves, crushed

a pinch of caster sugar

4 fresh basil leaves (optional)

sea salt and freshly ground black pepper

You can use vine-ripened tomatoes at the height of summer to make this sauce, but I normally buy the best tinned Italian plum tomatoes I can find – as a rule, the more expensive they are, the better they are! Make sure they are whole plum tomatoes and not chopped, which tend to be watery and disappointing. I use this as a tomato sauce for pasta, but any leftovers are also great spread onto a pizza base.

If you're using vine-ripened tomatoes, you'll need to peel and deseed them first. To peel a tomato, use a sharp knife to cut a cross at the base of the tomato, then put in a large heatproof bowl. Pour over boiling water and leave for a few seconds, until the skin near the cross starts to curl, then transfer to a bowl of cold water and peel off the skin. To remove the seeds, cut through the centre of the tomato, then cut into quarters. Using a small sharp knife, cut through the flesh at the top and pull out the seeds or use a teaspoon to scoop them out.

Heat the olive oil in a pan over a medium heat. Add the onion and garlic and cook for 2–3 minutes, until softened but not coloured, stirring occasionally with a wooden spoon.

Tip the tin of tomatoes or diced fresh tomatoes into the onion mixture and stir to combine. Add the sugar and season to taste with salt and pepper, then mash with a potato masher to break down the tomatoes. Reduce the heat and simmer gently for 5–6 minutes, until nicely reduced and slightly thickened. Blitz with a hand-held blender until smooth, then tear in the basil leaves if you're going to use the sauce immediately.

If you want to keep the sauce for up to a week in the fridge, transfer it to a Kilner jar or a bowl covered with cling film will also work. If you like the basil flavour, tear the leaves and stir them in just before using. →

NEVEN'S TOP TIP

Once you have mastered the basics, you can add other simple ingredients to the sauce that will transform the flavours. Try adding a finely chopped mild red chilli or ½ teaspoon of crushed chilli flakes with the onion and gar- lic if you want a tomato sauce with more of a kick. To take that one step further, add four finely chopped anchovies, 100g of pitted black olives and 3 tablespoons of rinsed capers for a much punchier flavour.

1

2

3

RAGÙ SAUCE

MAKES ABOUT 900ML (1½ PINTS)

2 tbsp olive or rapeseed oil

100g (4oz) pancetta or rindless smoked streaky bacon, very finely diced

1 onion, finely diced

1 large carrot, finely diced

1 celery stick, finely diced

1 large garlic clove, crushed

1 tsp fresh thyme leaves

1 bay leaf

350g (12oz) lean minced beef

200g (7oz) minced pork

150ml (¼ pint) white wine

3 heaped tbsp tomato purée

1 x 400g (14oz) tin of Italian whole plum tomatoes

2 tinned anchovy fillets, finely minced to a paste, or 1 tsp anchovy essence (optional)

6 tbsp milk

sea salt and freshly ground black pepper

Feel free to bulk this out with as much vegetables as you like or even add extra ones, such as mushrooms or courgettes. I also often add a tin of kidney beans or black beans with a scattering of fresh chilli flakes for a chilli con carne. I use this to make lasagne (page 61) or add it to some freshly cooked spaghetti for spaghetti Bolognese.
I like to add anchovies to it for a wonderfully subtle savoury note, but if you are unsure, leave them out and the ragù will still taste delicious.

Heat a large heavy-based pan over a medium heat. Add the oil, then tip in the pancetta or bacon. Cook for a couple of minutes, until crisp and the fat has rendered. Add the onion, carrot, celery, garlic, thyme and bay leaf with a pinch of salt and cook for about 10 minutes, stirring occasionally, until the vegetables have softened and taken on a little colour.

Add the beef and pork mince to the pan. Mix to combine, then sauté for about 5 minutes, until well browned and any liquid has bubbled away, breaking up any lumps with a wooden spoon. Add the white wine, scraping up any sediment from the bottom of the pan with a wooden spoon, then simmer until almost all of the liquid has evaporated. Stir in the tomato purée and cook, stirring, for a minute or two, until well combined.

Break up the plum tomatoes with your fingers and add to the pan with the anchovies or anchovy essence (if using), then season to taste with salt and pepper. Bring to the boil, then reduce the heat and simmer, stirring from time to time, for at least 1 hour or up to 2 hours is fine, until the beef is completely tender and the sauce is well reduced. It shouldn't be too wet. Stir in the milk about 15 minutes before the end of the cooking time so that it has time to reduce down a little. Season to taste. →

Use the ragù sauce at once or store in the fridge in a bowl covered with cling film for up to three days or freeze it in small batches to use when the need arises. Date and label the container or freezer bag before you freeze.

NEVEN'S TOP TIP

When I was in Bologna recently I tasted the most incredible ragù sauce. The secret ingredient? Roasted bone marrow. If you fancy giving it a try, ask your butcher for 2 x 5cm (2in) pieces of bone marrow. Towards the end of the simmering time, preheat the oven to 180°C (350°F/gas mark 4). Lightly season the marrow bones and put them in a roasting tin. Roast for 20 minutes, then scoop out the bone marrow with the end of a spoon and add it to the sauce with the milk.

1

2

3

BASIL PESTO
MAKES ABOUT 500ML (18FL OZ)

25g (1oz) pine nuts

200g (7oz) fresh basil

1 small garlic clove, peeled

300ml (½ pint) extra virgin olive oil, plus a little extra

50g (2oz) Parmesan cheese, freshly grated

sea salt and freshly ground black pepper

We have embraced pesto like it's our own, and although it has its uses as an ingredient, it's just wonderful folded into some freshly cooked linguine or as a dressing for green beans. It's very useful to have in the fridge, where it will keep happily for a week. Just keep it topped up with a little extra oil to keep it tasting lovely and fresh.

Put a heavy-based frying pan over a medium heat, then add the pine nuts. Toast until lightly golden, tossing them regularly to ensure that they cook evenly and don't burn. Remove from the heat and leave to cool completely. These help to thicken the pesto and toasting them before use really helps to bring out their flavour.

Pick the basil leaves off the stalks and place in a food processor. It's important not to use any of the stalks, as they discolour the pesto. Add the toasted pine nuts, garlic and a quarter of the oil to the food processor. Pulse gently until roughly chopped so that there is still some texture left in the nuts. Quickly pour in the remaining oil through the feeder tube. The quicker you manage to do this, the fresher the taste and the more aromatic the pesto (see the tip on the next page for more info).

Transfer the pesto to a bowl and fold in the Parmesan, then season to taste with salt and pepper. Cover with cling film or transfer to a clean jar and add a little extra oil on top to help prevent the pesto from discolouring. Keep in the fridge until needed and use as required. →

NEVEN'S TOP TIP

Basil is a very delicate herb, prone to wilting or turning black if roughly handled. Be careful not to overwork the mixture in the food processor – the longer you blend it, the darker it will look and the more in danger you are of it losing its wonderful aromatic character. For an intensely vibrant green colour, add a handful of baby spinach with the basil.

MUSHROOMS À LA CRÈME
MAKES ABOUT 450ML (¾ PINT)

25g (1oz) butter

2 shallots, finely chopped

225g (8oz) button mushrooms, trimmed and sliced

150ml (¼ pint) cream

squeeze of fresh lemon juice

1 tbsp chopped fresh flat-leaf parsley

1 tsp chopped fresh chives

sea salt and freshly ground black pepper

This is a version of the first sauce that I learned to make at college and I still make it to fold into pasta for a quick supper, perhaps sprinkling over some freshly grated Parmesan to serve. It's very versatile and can also be served with steak (page 163), pan-fried pork or lamb chops. It's fairly rich, so you don't need much of it – a little goes a long way.

Heat a frying pan over a medium heat. Add half the butter and swirl it around until it has melted and is foaming. Tip in the shallots and sauté for 2–3 minutes, until tender.

Add the rest of the butter to the pan, then tip in the mushrooms and season with salt and pepper. Sauté for another 5 minutes, until the mushrooms are cooked through and tender.

Pour the cream into the pan and allow to bubble down for a few minutes, until it has thickened to a sauce consistency. Add the lemon juice and herbs, stirring to combine. Season to taste and use immediately or allow to cool down completely and store in a bowl covered with cling film in the fridge for up to two days. Reheat gently in a pan when needed. →

NEVEN'S TOP TIP

Once you have mastered the basic sauce, experiment by first dry-frying 100g (4oz) of diced pancetta or streaky bacon until sizzling and the fat has started to render, then continue making the sauce as described above. This version would be particularly good with a chicken breast. I have even used it to fill savoury pancakes on Shrove Tuesday and it was delicious.

Mushrooms à la crème

BÉCHAMEL SAUCE

MAKES ABOUT 450ML (¾ PINT)

450ml (¾ pint) milk

1 onion, cut into thick slices

a few fresh parsley stalks

1 bay leaf

½ tsp black peppercorns

20g (¾oz) butter

20g (¾oz) plain flour

a pinch of freshly grated nutmeg

sea salt and freshly grated black pepper

This classic white sauce is the basis for so many dishes that it really is worth mastering, using what the French call a roux. I have included two simple variations, which give very different results. Béchamel is also essential for lasagne (page 61) and you'll need to make a double amount for a standard-sized dish.

Place the milk in a pan over a low heat. Add the onion, parsley stalks, bay leaf and peppercorns. Bring to the scalding point – this will take about 5 minutes – then remove from the heat, cover and set aside to infuse for at least 10 minutes and up to 30 minutes. Strain through a fine-mesh sieve into a jug.

Wipe out the pan and use it to melt the butter over a medium-low heat. Be careful not to overheat the butter or allow it to brown, as this will affect the colour and flavour of the sauce. Stir in the flour and cook for 1 minute, stirring quite vigorously to make a smooth, glossy paste (roux). Remove from the heat and gradually pour in the infused milk, whisking with a balloon whisk until smooth after each addition. Season to taste and add a pinch of freshly grated nutmeg.

Bring the sauce to the boil, whisking constantly, then reduce the heat and simmer gently for 5 minutes, stirring occasionally, until smooth and thickened. Use as required or transfer to a jug. If you want to keep the sauce warm, cover the surface with cling film to stop a skin from forming, then place the jug in a pan of barely simmering water. If using later, simply cover with cling film and keep in the fridge for up to two days. →

CHEESE SAUCE

This is great for broccoli and cauliflower gratin (page 171) or macaroni cheese. When the sauce is cooked, remove the pan from the heat and stir in 50g (2oz) of freshly grated Parmesan, mature Cheddar or Gruyère cheese until melted.

THICK BÉCHAMEL SAUCE

Although I have included how to make a sauce in the recipe for fish pie on page 115, this is effectively the consistency of thick sauce that you need. Increase the butter and flour to 40g (1½oz) each. If you would like a richer version, reduce the milk to 300ml (½ pint). Once the sauce has thickened, whisk in 150ml (¼ pint) of cream and allow to reduce and thicken a little. Stir in 2 tablespoons of chopped fresh flat-leaf parsley before using.

1

4

5

GRAVY
SERVES 4–6

roasting tin with vegetables left over from a roast (see the recipes on pages 128–142)

1 tbsp plain flour

100ml (3½fl oz) red or white wine or cider (a splash of sherry or port also works well)

500ml (18fl oz) beef, lamb or chicken stock (page 50 or use a made-up stock cube or water)

1–2 tsp redcurrant jelly (optional)

sea salt and freshly ground black pepper

I often get asked what the best way of making gravy is, so in this book I've decided to give it its very own recipe. After all, your Sunday roast is only as good as the gravy! In my opinion there are two things that are crucial to good gravy: roasting your joint on a trivet of vegetables and using the juices from the rested joint. If you do these two things, then even if you use water or a stock cube, you'll find that you've got a pretty good gravy.

To make the gravy, you'll need to have transferred your joint to a carving board and covered it with tin foil and a clean tea towel. Place the roasting tin with the trivet of roasted vegetables and meat or poultry juices on the hob and spoon off any excess fat, then add the flour and cook for 1 minute, stirring.

Using a potato masher, quickly mash the vegetables to release their flavour, then pour in the wine or cider. Allow to bubble down and reduce, scraping the bottom to remove any sediment. Gradually add the stock or water and bring to the boil, continuously scraping the bottom of the tin to ensure you get all the flavour.

Reduce the heat and simmer for 5 minutes, then pass through a fine-mesh sieve into a small clean pan. Season to taste and whisk in the redcurrant jelly if you think it would benefit from a little sweetness. Pour into a warmed gravy boat to serve. →

Keep any leftover gravy in a ziplock bag in the freezer and use it when you don't have time to make gravy or to add to one that you feel is lacking a bit in flavour, perhaps because you haven't had time to create the depth of flavour with a trivet of vegetables.

1

4

SALAD DRESSING

MAKES ABOUT 175ML (6FL OZ)

2 tbsp white or red wine vinegar

1 tsp honey

8 tbsp extra virgin rapeseed oil

1 tsp Dijon mustard

sea salt and freshly ground black pepper

At home I always make salad dressing in a screw-topped jar (a clean old jam jar) so that it can be left in the fridge and shaken up as I need it. I like to use an extra virgin rapeseed oil in my dressing as we love the taste and it's great to be supporting Irish producers and farmers. However, the type of oil you use is a personal preference, as it has a big impact on the flavour of the dressing, so experiment until you learn what you like best.

Put the vinegar in a screw-topped jar with a pinch of salt and the honey. Shake until the salt and honey have dissolved.

Add the oil and mustard along with some black pepper and shake again until emulsified. The ratio of a good salad dressing is three parts oil to one part acid (vinegar or lemon), but it's always sensible to have a little taste. If the seasoning is there but you're finding it a little too acidic, you've got the right balance, because once the dressing is on the salad leaves it will be perfect. →

NEVEN'S TOP TIP – NO TIME TO MAKE DRESSING?

Sometimes you just want to dress a salad instantly, and as long as you've got a good extra virgin olive oil and some aged balsamic vinegar, you will never go wrong. Simply drizzle a little oil all over your salad, followed by about half the amount of the balsamic, then use your fingers to toss lightly to coat (see page 24 on how to dress a salad).

SALSA

This salsa really comes into its own in the summer, although if you are using tropical fruit, salsa certainly has a place all year round. Salsa is quick and easy to prepare and goes with everything from nibbles to barbecued meat, fish and seafood. Everything should be hand chopped, so no shortcuts in a food processor will do! Choose one ingredient from each row on pages 200–201, then play around with the flavour to suit your own tastes.

Prepare the fruit and cut the flesh into rough 5mm (¼in) dice, discarding any seeds or stones, and put in a bowl. Finely chop the onion or a few spring onions and add those. Add a squeeze of citrus juice or vinegar and season with a pinch of salt. If using chilli, deseed and finely chop it or crush the garlic and gradually add until you achieve the desired flavour. It's important to taste the salsa at this point.

Let the prepared salsa sit at room temperature for up to 30 minutes, but don't be tempted to make it too far ahead, as salsas rely on freshness of flavour.

When ready to serve, give it a good stir and fold in the chopped fresh herb of your choice, adding another squeeze of citrus juice or vinegar, a little more chilli or garlic or another pinch of salt if you think it needs it. →

NEVEN'S TOP TIP

This salsa is so simple that it stands or falls on the ripeness of the fruit, so make sure that the one you choose is going to do it justice and never use specimens that are past their best. Look for fruit that seems aromatic but is still nice and firm so that the flesh will be easy to chop.

FRUIT

Mango

Tomatoes

Pineapple

AROMATICS

Red onion

Spring onions

Sweet white onions

CITRUS/ACID

Lime

Lemon

White wine vinegar

FLAVOUR ADD-INS

Red chilli

Green chilli

Garlic

HERBS

Coriander

Mint

Basil

GUACAMOLE
MAKES ABOUT 300ML (½ PINT)

3 firm ripe avocados (preferably Hass)

1 fresh green chilli

2 spring onions

15g (½oz) fresh coriander

1 ripe tomato

juice of 1 lime

sea salt and freshly ground black pepper

A good guacamole should be zingy and fresh-tasting to cut through the rich creaminess of the avocado. The exact amount of the ingredients you use can be played around with according to taste. The only golden rule is to use firm, ripe avocados. I think that the Hass variety, which are the knobbly brown ones, tend to be consistently the most flavoursome and creamiest. Serve with tacos, fajitas or with some tortilla chips as a dip.

Cut the avocados in half and remove the stones, then peel off the skin. Cut the flesh into dice and put into a bowl. Mash into a chunky paste with a fork, leaving some pieces intact.

Cut the chilli in half and remove the seeds if you don't like things too hot, then finely chop the flesh and add to the mashed avocados.

Trim the spring onions. Pick the leaves off the coriander, then finely chop the spring onions and coriander together using a large sharp knife.

To remove the seeds from the tomato, cut through the centre of the tomato, then cut into quarters. Using a small sharp knife, cut through the flesh at the top and pull out the seeds or use a teaspoon to scoop them out, then finely dice the flesh.

Add the spring onions, coriander and tomato to the avocado mixture with the lime juice and mix well to combine. Season to taste with salt and pepper. Serve immediately or cover the surface with cling film and chill until needed (see the tip on the next page). →

Contrary to popular belief, popping an avocado stone into guacamole does not delay discolouration. The only thing that slows down the browning process is to exclude the air from it, which means pressing a piece of cling film down tightly directly on the surface before putting it into the fridge for up to 2 hours.

1

2

3

4

BÉARNAISE SAUCE

MAKES ABOUT 450ML (¾ PINT)

2 egg yolks

1 egg

2 tsp tarragon or white wine vinegar

1 tsp chopped fresh tarragon

a pinch of salt

225g (8oz) unsalted butter, diced

This classic sauce is wonderful served with a steak (page 103) or, if you're lucky enough to have some, trout or poached wild salmon.

Place the egg yolks, egg, vinegar, fresh tarragon and salt in a food processor. Blend until the tarragon is very finely chopped.

Gently heat the butter in a heavy-based pan until melted and just beginning to foam. Turn on the food processor. With the motor running at medium speed, pour in the melted butter through the feeder tube in a thin, steady stream. Leave any milky sediment in the bottom of the pan behind. Continue to blitz for another 5 seconds, then pour back into the pan but don't return to the heat.

Allow the heat from the pan to finish thickening the sauce as you stir it gently for another minute before serving. Alternatively, the sauce can be kept warm in a heatproof bowl set over a pan of simmering water or in a switched-off but warm oven. →

NEVEN'S TOP TIP

Omit the vinegar and tarragon and you've got hollandaise sauce, which is great ladled over split buttered muffins, topped with hand-carved glazed ham (page 119) and poached eggs (page 7).

1

2

WHOLEMEAL SOURDOUGH
MAKES 1 LOAF

FOR THE STARTER:

50g (2oz) wholegrain rye flour

50g (2oz) strong white flour

150ml (¼ pint) warm water

25g (1oz) rhubarb, very thinly sliced (on a mandolin is perfect)

FOR THE DAILY FEED FOR DAYS 2 TO 4:

25g (1oz) wholegrain rye flour

25g (1oz) strong white flour

50ml (1½fl oz) warm water

FOR THE DAILY FEED FOR DAYS 5 AND 6:

125ml (4¼fl oz) warm water

75g (3oz) strong white flour

40g (1½oz) wholegrain rye flour

30g (1¼oz) wholemeal flour

FOR THE DOUGH:

375g (13oz) strong white flour, plus extra for dusting

250g (9oz) starter

1 tsp fine sea salt

120–175ml (4–6fl oz) warm water

olive oil, for kneading and greasing

With a sourdough starter kept handy in the fridge, tasty, chewy bread can be yours on demand. It will take about a week to create, but with care and regular feeding it can last you a lifetime. I use rhubarb to help kick-start the fermentation, as it has plenty of natural yeast and always gives a successful result. On Day 5 of the process you will need to discard the leftover starter or pass it on to someone else to make their own. French bannetons – the woven, cloth-lined baskets traditionally used to prove bread – can be very expensive to buy, but a similar-sized wicker basket (approximately 24cm/9½in) lined with a linen tea towel also works well, as it allows for air circulation.

DAY ONE
To make the starter, mix the flours in a bowl with your hands until combined. Put the water in a large Kilner jar or bowl with the rhubarb and use your hands to mix in the flours until it resembles a thick paste. Wrap this jar or bowl loosely in cling film and leave in a warm place for 24 hours.

DAY TWO
At around the same time the following day, mix the first batch of the daily feed, which is simply the flours and water, into your starter and leave somewhere warm, again loosely covered with cling film. If there is a bit of skin on top, just mix it in.

DAY THREE
Repeat as per Day 2.

DAY FOUR
By now you should start seeing active fermentation. Repeat as per Day 2.

DAY FIVE
The starter should be bubbling away and smell tangy. Mix it to combine, then put 30g (1¼oz) of the starter into a larger bowl. Pick out any pieces of rhubarb and discard. Whisk in the water and stir in the flours until well combined. Cover loosely with

1

2

3   Starter Days 2-4

4   Starter Days 5-6

Sourdough starter

cling film and leave in a warm place for 24 hours. You don't need the rest of the starter now, so you could gift it to friends and family if they'd like to have a go at making their own sourdough too or use it to make pancakes (page 15), pizzas (page 109) or scones (page 237) for a lovely tang.

DAY SIX

Repeat as per Day 5, again using only 30g (1 ¼ oz) of the starter.

DAY SEVEN

Now you can finally make your bread. To make the dough, combine the flour, starter and salt in a large bowl. Add the water a little at a time and mix with your hands to make a soft dough – you may not need all of the water.

Coat the work surface in a little olive oil, then tip the dough onto it and knead for 10–15 minutes, until smooth and elastic. Tip into a lightly oiled bowl and cover with cling film. Leave to rise in a warm place for 5 hours, until it has at least doubled in size.

Tip the dough back onto the work surface and knead again until smooth, knocking most of the air out. Roll into a ball and dust with flour. Put into a well-floured round banneton or proving basket (see the intro), then cover with a clean tea towel and place in a cool, not cold, place and leave to rise slowly for 8 hours.

Put a roasting tin half-filled with water on the bottom shelf of the oven and preheat to 220°C (425°F/gas mark 7). Dust a baking sheet gener-ously with flour.

Gently tip the risen dough out of the basket onto the baking sheet. Using a small sharp knife, cut a cross into the top of the dough. Bake in the oven for 30 minutes, then reduce the oven temperature to 200°C (400°F/gas mark 6) and bake for another 15–20 minutes, until the loaf is golden brown, the outside crust is crisp and the bread sounds hollow when tapped on the base. Transfer the loaf to a wire rack and leave to cool for at least 1 hour before slicing and serving. →

If you are using your starter often, you can leave it at room temperature, feeding it at least every three days and whenever you take some to make bread. Simply stir in some strong white flour and enough water to return it to the consistency of very wet dough, bearing in mind that you will need about 375g (13oz) of starter for each loaf of bread. Then leave it, covered, until it achieves that thick, bubbly, jelly-like stage. If you are making sourdough less often – say, once a month – then keep the starter covered in the fridge. This will slow down the activity and preserve it almost indefinitely, but you must let it come back to room temperature before use. If it ever seems inactive, give it a feed of strong white flour – the bacteria within it are living, so they need feeding.

1

Snacks and

Teatime

OATMEAL CHOCOLATE CHIP COOKIES
MAKES ABOUT 36

275g (10oz) Flahavan's Progress Oatlets

225g (8oz) butter, softened

150g (5oz) caster sugar

100g (4oz) plain flour, plus a little extra for dusting

½ tsp bicarbonate of soda

100g (4oz) plain or milk chocolate chips

I love oatmeal cookies and these ones are particularly delicious with the chocolate chips. The cookie rolls keep well in the fridge for up to one week or can be frozen and defrosted at room temperature before using. Once baked, the cookies keep well in an airtight container for up to one week.

Blend the oatlets in a food processor until quite fine. Add the butter, sugar, flour and bicarbonate of soda and blend again until the dough just comes together. Fold in the chocolate chips.

Divide the dough into three pieces and roll each one into a long sausage shape that is 15cm (6in) long and 4cm (1½in) wide. Wrap in cling film and chill in the fridge for 1 hour to firm up.

Preheat the oven to 180°C (350°F/gas mark 4). Line two baking sheets with non-stick baking paper.

Using a sharp knife, trim the ends from each cookie roll, then cut each roll into about 12 cookies – in other words, each cookie should be a little more than 1cm (½in) thick.

Arrange the cookies well-spaced apart on the lined baking sheets. Bake in the oven for 15–20 minutes, until pale golden and slightly firm.

Remove from the oven and leave to cool for a minute, then transfer to a wire rack and leave to cool completely. Put into Kilner jars or arrange on a plate to serve. →

If you prefer a more chewy cookie, the trick is to take them out of the oven before they are super firm – you want them to be slightly under-baked so that they are still chewy when they cool, although this cookie is particularly good when still warm.

1

2

3

4

5

SCONES
MAKES 8–10

225g (8oz) self-raising flour, plus extra for dusting

a pinch of fine sea salt

a pinch of baking powder

40g (1½oz) caster sugar, plus extra for sprinkling

75g (3oz) butter, diced

1 large egg, lightly beaten

3 tbsp buttermilk, plus a little extra

TO SERVE

butter

whipped cream

raspberry jam

If I made a list of my top ten foods, a freshly baked scone would be on there: so simple, but soft, fluffy and a taste of home. These scones should take you no more than 15 minutes to get in the oven, so you'll have them on the table in less than half an hour. They don't keep well, so in the unlikely event that there are any left, pop them in the freezer. I often freeze the raw scone and bake it for 15 minutes from frozen.

Preheat the oven to 220°C (425°F/gas mark 7).

Sift the flour into a bowl with the salt and baking powder, then stir in the sugar and rub in the butter. The best way to do this is to pick the mixture up with your fingertips and lightly rub it together before letting it fall back into the bowl. Repeat this until the mixture resembles fine breadcrumbs. You can also use a food processor to do this, although I never bother.

Beat the egg with the buttermilk. Make a well in the centre of the dry ingredients. Using a palette knife, gently and quickly stir the liquid into the flour. When it begins to come together, finish it with your hands – the dough should be soft but not sticky. If the mixture seems a little dry, add a bit more buttermilk, 1 teaspoon at a time.

Lightly flour the work surface. Turn the dough out onto it and pat into a circle about 2.5cm (1in) thick. Be very careful not to roll it any thinner: the secret to a well-risen scone is to start out with a thickness no less than 2.5cm (1in). Cut into triangles with a sharp knife or stamp into 5cm (2in) rounds with a cutter, giving it a sharp tap – don't twist it, just lift it up and push the dough out. Carry on until you are left with all the trimmings, then bring these back together to roll out again until you can cut out the last scone.

Arrange the scones on a baking sheet lined with non-stick baking paper and brush the tops with buttermilk, then sprinkle with a little more sugar. →

Bake in the oven for 10–12 minutes, until well-risen and golden brown. Leave to cool for at least 10 minutes on a wire rack.

These scones are best served warm and straight out of the oven. Serve with butter for spreading and small pots of whipped cream and raspberry jam.

NEVEN'S TOP TIP

For a savoury option try making cheese and pancetta scones, which would be delicious with soup or as a midmorning snack. Omit the sugar and add a pinch of dry mustard powder and paprika with the flour. Once the butter has been rubbed in, add 100g (4oz) of pancetta that has been dry-fried until crisp and drained of any excess oil along with 50g (2oz) of grated mature Cheddar cheese and 1 tablespoon of snipped fresh chives. Once the scones are glazed and ready to go into the oven, sprinkle the tops with a little more grated cheese.

3

4

CUSTARD
MAKES ABOUT 400ML (14FL OZ)

5 egg yolks

3 tbsp caster sugar

½ vanilla pod, split in half lengthways and seeds scraped out

300ml (½ pint) milk

100ml (3½fl oz) cream

This is a perfect pouring custard for a fruit crumble (page 77) or apple tart (page 111). The yolks give a richer-tasting, velvety custard, while adding the whole egg helps to stabilise it a bit more for a slightly more sturdy custard. It is not a sauce to attempt in a rush, so if you're pressed for time it's probably best to use a fresh ready-made custard, such as Dunnes Stores Simply Better Madagascan Vanilla Bean Custard. However, once made it will keep in the fridge for up to three days.

Place the egg yolks in a large bowl with the sugar and vanilla seeds. Whisk with an electric mixer for a few minutes, until pale and thickened.

Place the milk and cream in a medium-sized heavy-based pan and bring to the boil, then immediately remove from the heat.

Gradually whisk the heated milk and cream into the egg yolk mixture until smooth, then pour everything back into the pan and place over a medium heat. Cook gently for 6–8 minutes, stirring constantly, until the custard coats the back of a wooden spoon or spatula. The longer you cook it, the thicker it will get.

Serve the custard hot or transfer to a jug. Cover the surface with cling film to help prevent a skin from forming and leave to cool, then chill in the fridge until needed. It can also be put into a squeezy bottle depending on how you want to use it. Use hot or cold as required. →

NEVEN'S TOP TIP

For a grown-up kick, add 2 tablespoons of Coole Swan Irish Cream Liqueur to the custard before it gets cooked to thicken.

1

4

5

Bread

BROWN SODA BREAD
MAKES 1 LOAF

rapeseed oil, for greasing

225g (8oz) strong white flour, plus extra for dusting

225g (8oz) wholemeal flour

1 tsp bicarbonate of soda

2 tsp light muscovado sugar

1 tsp fine sea salt

450ml (¾ pint) buttermilk, plus extra if needed

1 heaped tbsp sunflower seeds

2 tsp melted butter, plus extra for spreading to serve

1 tsp golden syrup

a handful of porridge oats

1 heaped tsp pumpkin seeds

1 heaped tsp sesame seeds

Otherwise known as wheaten bread, this is a recipe that's close to my heart, as it has taken me years to perfect. It's a great bread for novice cooks to start with as there is no proving or kneading, as the bicarbonate is responsible for the rise when it reacts with the buttermilk. If you don't have any buttermilk in the house, sour ordinary milk with the juice of a lemon or 3 tablespoons of red wine vinegar, which gives the bread a little more tang. It literally goes with everything but is particularly good with soup or cut into slices and served with smoked salmon.

Preheat the oven to 200°C (400°F/gas mark 6). Lightly oil a 600g (1lb 5oz) loaf tin.

Sift the flours and bicarbonate of soda into a large bowl, then tip in any remaining bran left behind in the sieve. Stir in the muscovado sugar and salt. Make a well in the centre and add the buttermilk, sunflower seeds, melted butter and golden syrup. Using a large spoon, mix gently and quickly until you have achieved a nice dropping consistency. Add a little more buttermilk if necessary until the dough binds together without being sloppy.

Put the mixture into the prepared loaf tin and sprinkle over the porridge oats, pumpkin and sesame seeds. Bake in the oven for 40 minutes, until cooked through and the loaf has a slightly cracked, crusty top, checking halfway through the cooking time to make sure that it isn't browning too much. If it is, reduce the temperature or move the loaf down in the oven.

To check that the loaf is properly cooked, tip it out of the tin and tap the base – it should sound hollow. If it doesn't, return it to the oven for another 5 minutes. Tip out onto a wire rack and leave to cool completely. →

To serve, place the brown soda bread on a bread-board and cut into slices at the table. Hand around with a separate pot of butter for spreading.

If you prefer a lighter brown soda bread, simply use about three-quarters strong white bread flour to one-quarter wholemeal and add 25g (1oz) of pinhead oatmeal before adding the buttermilk. I also try to use a coarse wholemeal flour, which will give your bread a lovely nutty flavour and nubbly texture.

1

4

WHITE LOAF
MAKES 1 LOAF

rapeseed oil, for greasing

500g (18oz) strong white flour, plus extra for dusting

1 x 7g (¼oz) sachet of fast-action dried yeast, about 1 tbsp in total

1 tsp fine sea salt

about 350ml (12fl oz) hand-hot water

Once you have mastered this classic white loaf, the bread-making world is your oyster! This loaf will stay fresh in an airtight container or wrapped tightly in tin foil for up to three days or can be frozen for up to one month.

Lightly grease a 900g (2lb) loaf tin.

Place the flour in a large bowl with the yeast and salt. Stir to combine, then make a well in the centre and pour in most of the water. Quickly mix it with your fingers for 2–3 minutes, then knead to incorporate the flour, scraping the sides of the bowl and folding the dough over itself until it gathers into a rough mass. The dough should feel slightly wet and pillowy but workable. If it doesn't, add a splash more water if necessary.

Turn the dough out onto a well-floured surface and lightly flour your hands. Knead for at least 10 minutes, until the dough is smooth and pliable. The dough will be very sticky at first, so keep your hands and the work surface lightly floured to prevent it from sticking and building up on the work surface. As you continue kneading, the dough will become more elastic and easier to handle.

Shape into a loose ball, then return it to an oiled bowl and cover with cling film. Leave to rest in a warm, draught-free place for 1 hour or until doubled in size.

Turn the dough out again onto a lightly floured surface and knock it back by tipping it back and pushing the air out. Knead the dough for a few seconds, until it becomes springy and smooth. The gas bubbles will be redistributed so the final loaf has an even-textured crumb.

Shape the dough into a rectangular ball using the length of the prepared tin as a rough guide. Place in the prepared tin, smoothing down the sides. Cover with a clean tea towel and leave to prove in a warm place for another 30 minutes, until slightly risen. Dust the top of the loaf with a little more flour and slash with a sharp knife if you want. Meanwhile, preheat the oven to 220°C (425°F/gas mark 7).

Bake the loaf in the oven for 15 minutes, then reduce the heat to 190°C (375°F/gas mark 5) and continue to bake for 30 minutes more, until the loaf is a deep golden brown. To check that the loaf is done, carefully tip the loaf out of the tin using oven gloves and rap the underside with your knuckles. If the loaf sounds hollow, like a drum, it's done. If you just get a dull thud, return the loaf to the oven, putting it straight on the oven shelf, and bake for another 5 minutes, then test again. Transfer the bread to a wire rack to cool completely before cutting into slices.

NEVEN'S TOP TIP

Once you have mastered the basic recipe, the dough can be flavoured with 1 tablespoon of chopped fresh herbs, such as thyme or rosemary. For a more pronounced taste, add up to 4 tablespoons of chopped fresh mixed herbs, such as a mixture of flat-leaf parsley, basil and chives. For a completely different flavour, try adding 2 tablespoons of basil pesto (page 183).

VANILLA CUPCAKES
MAKES 12

175g (6oz) butter, softened

175g (6oz) light muscovado sugar

4 eggs

3 tbsp buttermilk or sour cream

seeds of ½ vanilla pod or 1 tsp vanilla extract

225g (8oz) self-raising flour

½ tsp bicarbonate of soda

FOR THE CREAM CHEESE FROSTING

500g (18oz) icing sugar

175g (6oz) butter, softened

100g (4oz) cream cheese

seeds of 1 vanilla pod or 2 tsp vanilla extract

This is a great cupcake recipe that has a sweet and slightly sour cream cheese frosting. I promise that if you make them they are always going to be a big hit. The hardest thing to do is trying to figure out how not to eat them all before you take them to whoever you have made them for!

Preheat the oven to 180°C (350°F/gas mark 4). Line a muffin tin with 12 paper cases.

Put the butter and sugar in a bowl and beat well. The best way to do this is with a hand-held electric whisk. The mixture should become a little lighter in colour. Add two of the eggs along with buttermilk or sour cream, vanilla and half of the flour and beat well to just combine. Add the other two eggs and the rest of the flour along with the bicarbonate of soda. Mix so that everything is just combined. Overmixing at this stage can result in tough cupcakes, so easy does it.

Divide the batter between the paper cases. I like to use an ice cream scoop to do this, but if you don't have one, then use two large spoons. Place the tin in the oven on the middle shelf and bake for 25–30 minutes, until the cupcakes are cooked. To test, insert a skewer into the centre of a cupcake and it should come out clean. The cupcakes will also smell cooked and be springy to the touch. Remove them from the oven and leave them to cool completely on a wire rack. The cupcakes must be completely cool before you ice them, otherwise the icing will melt.

While the cupcakes are cooling down, put the icing sugar, butter, cream cheese and vanilla in a bowl and mix together just enough to combine. Mix this with as few 'stirs' as possible because if the cream cheese is overmixed the frosting can become thin in consistency. Spoon or pipe the cream cheese frosting over the cooled cupcakes to serve. →

These days everyone seems to go wild for red velvet cupcakes. This recipe can be easily adjusted to make them. Simply use 25g (1oz) of cocoa powder instead of the equivalent amount of flour and add ½ teaspoon of red food colouring (Sugarflair is a good brand) after adding the bicarbonate of soda.

CHOCOLATE CAKE
SERVES 8–10

350g (12oz) light muscovado sugar

200g (7oz) butter, softened

seeds of ½ vanilla pod or ½ tsp vanilla extract

1 tbsp coffee essence (optional)

6 eggs, at room temperature

300g (11oz) self-raising flour

50g (2oz) good-quality cocoa powder

½ tsp baking powder

200g (7oz) crème fraîche, at room temperature

FOR THE CHOCOLATE FROSTING

100g (4oz) plain chocolate, broken into squares

350g (12oz) icing sugar, sifted

175g (6oz) butter, softened

2 tbsp cream

FOR THE CHOCOLATE GANACHE

150ml (¼ pint) cream

150g (5oz) plain chocolate, broken into squares

This is a super indulgent chocolate cake that is a perfect family treat and a real crowd pleaser, particularly for a birthday celebration. Try decorating it with Cadbury's mini eggs for Easter or for Christmas use a box of luxury chocolate truffles. The sponge is rich and moist and gets layered up with fudge-like chocolate icing before being covered in a layer of chocolate ganache. It's so rich that a little goes a long way. My mum always said that if you are going to treat yourself, do it properly! Sometimes feeling good is about pure indulgence, and chocolate is sure to hit the spot.

Preheat the oven to 180°C (350°F/gas mark 4). Line 2 x 20cm (8in) non-stick cake tins with non-stick baking paper.

Cream the sugar and butter together in a large bowl with a wooden spoon (or using a freestanding electric mixer) until light and fluffy. Add the vanilla seeds or extract along with the coffee essence (if using) and two of the eggs, then beat like mad again. Add another two eggs and continue to beat. The mixture may look less than perfect at this stage, but keep going and it will come good. Add the last two eggs and beat well again.

Sift together the flour, cocoa powder and baking powder. Using a large metal spoon, fold the dry ingredients into the creamed mixture in alternate batches with the crème fraîche. Mix well between each addition, scraping down the sides of the bowl with a rubber spatula.

Using the spatula, divide the batter evenly between the prepared tins, smoothing down the tops. Bake in the oven for 25–30 minutes, until the cakes are springy to the touch and a skewer inserted into the middle of each one of them comes out clean. Cool for 5 minutes in the tins, then turn out onto a wire rack and leave to cool completely. The cakes must be completely cool before you ice them, otherwise the icing will melt. →

When the cakes have cooled down completely, make the chocolate frosting. Melt the chocolate in a heatproof bowl set over a pan of simmering water, making sure the bottom of the bowl doesn't touch the water. Leave to cool a little, then mix with the rest of the chocolate frosting ingredients. I put them all in my freestanding electric mixer with a paddle attachment and beat it for a good 5 minutes, until it's light and spreadable, but it can also be done by hand.

Place one of the cakes on a plate or cake stand with a blob of frosting underneath so that the cake doesn't move, then spread the top with a little more frosting. Cover with more frosting, then top with the remaining cake, flipping it over so that the flat side of the cake is now at the top, giving a good flat base for the frosting. Lightly press the cake layers together, then use a palette knife to spread the remaining frosting evenly over the top and sides of the cake so that the sides are nice and straight and the top is flat. I like to do a thin layer first, which is called the crumb layer. If you have room in your freezer, place the cake in the freezer for 10 minutes for the layer to firm up.

Take the cake out of the freezer and add another, thicker layer of frosting. Have a good play around with the knife so that the frosting is really smooth. Sometimes it helps to run the palette knife under the warm tap and then carry on smoothing the frosting. Leave to set a little while you make the ganache drizzle.

Heat the cream in a pan but don't boil it. You want it to be just steaming. Take the pan off the heat and add the chocolate, leaving it to melt for a few minutes. Stir the chocolate gently and let it cool down a little. Pour the chocolate ganache over the cake so that it drizzles in a nice smooth layer all over the top and comes nicely down the sides of the cake. Leave to set at room temperature for at least 1 hour or overnight is fine. Serve with a flourish!

NEVEN'S TOP TIP

Sometimes icing a cake like this can seem like a daunting prospect, but if you give yourself plenty of time and stick to a couple of basic rules, it's a lot easier than you think. It's important to always flip the top cake over so that you end up with a good flat base for frosting the top and sides. For a clean finish, don't press down too much on the cakes, as this can cause the frosting to bulge out between each layer. Then follow the instructions in this recipe and you can't go far wrong.

VICTORIA SPONGE WITH LEMON CURD
SERVES 6–8

225g (8oz) butter, softened

200g (7oz) caster sugar

4 eggs

225g (8oz) self-raising flour

finely grated rind of 1 lemon

seeds of ½ vanilla pod or 1 tsp vanilla extract

¼ tsp baking powder

FOR THE BUTTERCREAM

200g (7oz) icing sugar, sifted

100g (4oz) butter, softened

seeds of ½ vanilla pod or 1 tsp vanilla extract

a drop of milk (if necessary)

FOR THE FILLING

7 tbsp shop-bought lemon curd

icing sugar, to dust

This is a slight twist on a classic Victoria sponge, but if you want to keep it traditional, then omit the lemon rind in the sponge and replace the lemon curd with your favourite strawberry jam.

Preheat the oven to 180°C (350°F/gas mark 4). Line 2 x 20cm (8in) loose-bottomed cake tins with non-stick baking paper.

Put the butter and sugar into a large bowl and cream together. I find the best way to do this is to use a wooden spoon to push the mixture onto the side of the bowl until it's mixed together, then beat it hard until the mixture turns from yellow to a paler shade. Alternatively, use a hand-held electric mixer or a freestanding electric mixer, which is much easier and quicker.

Add two of the eggs to the butter mixture along with half of the flour and beat together until combined. Add the other two eggs and the rest of the flour along with the lemon zest, vanilla and baking powder and beat like mad to get a good amount of air into it.

Divide the batter between the prepared cake tins and bake in the oven for 25–30 minutes, until the cakes have shrunk slightly from the sides of the tin, spring back when touched in the centre and a skewer inserted into the centre of each one comes out clean. Once baked, remove from the oven and leave the cakes to cool completely in the tins.

While the cakes are cooling, make the buttercream. Cream together the icing sugar, butter and vanilla in a bowl until light and fluffy, adding a drop of milk to loosen it if necessary.

Once the cakes are completely cool, place one on a cake stand and spread the buttercream on top, followed by the lemon curd. Cover with the other cake and dust with icing sugar to serve. →

NEVEN'S TOP TIP

To make this into a coffee cake, simply add 3 tablespoons of coffee essence to the batter with the vanilla and add another couple of teaspoons to the buttercream. Or try filling the sponge with a chocolate hazelnut spread instead of the lemon curd.

1

4

Desserts

RICE PUDDING
SERVES 4–6

500ml (18fl oz) milk

200ml (7fl oz) cream

100g (4oz) short-grain pudding rice

75g (3oz) caster sugar

25g (1oz) butter

½ vanilla pod, split in half lengthways, or 1 tsp vanilla extract

TO SERVE

raspberry jam (optional)

This is a wonderfully creamy rice pudding. For a low-fat version I use 750ml (1¼ pints) of semi-skimmed milk instead of the milk and cream or sometimes I replace 400ml (14fl oz) of the milk with a tin of coconut milk. My twins, Connor and Lucia, have loved this since they were little and it is certainly one of my all-time favourite desserts too.

Place the milk and cream in a heavy-based pan over a medium heat and bring to a simmer. Stir in the rice, sugar, butter and vanilla pod or extract and bring to the boil, stirring until the sugar has dissolved.

Reduce the heat to the lowest setting and cook for 30–40 minutes, until the rice is tender and creamy, stirring frequently to ensure it doesn't catch on the bottom. Remove the vanilla pod from the pan and discard.

Spoon the rice pudding into warmed bowls and add a little raspberry jam, if liked, to serve.

NEVEN'S TOP TIP

A bowl of warm rice pudding can also be made into a more sophisticated dessert with the addition of roasted pineapple or sautéed bananas and a drizzle of caramel sauce, or really any stewed fruit (see page 257–258). A dollop of your favourite jam is also a good option.

Rice pudding

STEWED FRUIT
MAKES 675G (1½LB)

750g (1lb 10oz) seasonal fruit, such as Bramley apples, rhubarb, plums, apricots or pears

2 heaped tbsp caster sugar, plus a little extra if necessary

2 tbsp water

Stewed fruit is great with cereal and/or yogurt or even just on its own with custard (page 211) or to serve with pancakes (page 15), waffles or French toast. It makes the perfect base for a crumble (page 77) or a single-crust pie (page 111). It's also brilliant with meringues (page 265) or maybe some chocolate sauce (page 261) – the possibilities are endless! Whatever your desire, it's wonderful to have your freezer filled with seasonal fruit ready to come to the rescue (see the tip on the next page).

Peel the apples (if using) and roughly chop up all the fruit, discarding any stones or cores. Put the fruit in a pan with the caster sugar and water and put on a medium heat with the lid on. Cook gently until the fruit has just started to soften. Remove the lid and continue to cook gently until the fruit is just tender but is still holding its shape.

Taking the lid off will allow the liquid to reduce a bit, but try not to stir it too much or you'll end up with a purée. Remove from the heat and leave to cool slightly. Taste the stewed fruit – if you think it's too tart, stir in a little more caster sugar to taste. →

NEVEN'S TOP TIP

Most fruit freezes well and can be stored, frozen, for six months and even up to a year. Inevitably some deterioration will occur, but with the correct care it can be kept to a minimum. To freeze berries or firm ripe fruit that doesn't need to be cooked, spread it out on a tray lined with parchment paper in a single layer that's not touching and put in the freezer. Once frozen, transfer it to polythene freezer bags. Alternatively, if you're planning to use it in a tart or crumble, make the fruit filling as described on the previous page. The sugar will absorb the juice that runs from the fruit when it becomes syrupy upon defrosting. Apples and rhubarb freeze very well, but stoned fruits usually become very soft once thawed. An exception is strawberries, which turn to mush when you defrost them.

MIXED FRUIT FLAVOUR COMBINATIONS

Many fruits have natural partners and here are some of my favourites that are perfect for a crumble or pie filling. If they need to be stewed, simply fold them together gently before using. Soft berries can be used raw with no need to cook them first.
- Stewed apple and cranberry or blackberry
- Stewed rhubarb and plum or strawberry
- Stewed mango and blueberry
- Stewed pear and raspberry or fig
- Stewed gooseberry and elderflower

1

2

CHOCOLATE SAUCE
MAKES ABOUT 250ML (9FL OZ)

120ml (4fl oz) cream

25g (1oz) caster sugar

25g (1oz) butter

50g (2oz) plain chocolate, finely chopped (at least 70% cocoa solids) or plain chocolate chips

Who doesn't like a rich, smooth chocolate sauce? Use it to make the ultimate ice cream sundae, a banana split, spooned onto cherries or to flavour milk for a wonderfully decadent hot chocolate. This is one recipe where only a good-quality plain chocolate will do, as a chocolate sauce made with milk chocolate is just too sweet for most palates. This will keep happily for up to one week covered with cling film in the fridge.

Place the cream in a pan over a medium heat. Add the sugar and butter and bring to the boil, stirring. Reduce the heat and simmer gently for 2–3 minutes, until thickened and beginning to become syrupy, stirring occasionally to prevent the mixture from catching. Remove from the heat and add the chocolate. Set aside to allow it to melt, then whisk until smooth.

This is now ready to serve warm or else you can transfer it to a bowl and leave to cool completely, then cover with cling film and keep in the fridge until needed. Use warm or cold as required. →

Rich, sweet and chocolatey, this sauce is perfect just as it
is, although I sometimes add a small pinch of flaky sea salt
or a splash of Coole Swan Irish Cream Liqueur. My favourite
way of having it is with a couple scoops of vanilla ice cream
adorned with a few cherries on top.

1

4

2

3

5

6

MERINGUES
MAKES 12

½ lemon

4 egg whites, at room temperature (see the tip on the next page for more info)

225g (8oz) caster sugar

1 tsp cornflour (optional – see intro)

TO SERVE

softly whipped cream

fresh berries or sliced summer fruits, such as peaches or plums

fresh mint sprigs

Some people find meringues difficult to make, but I hope this recipe makes it easy! It just takes a good recipe, some eggs that are about a week old (but still in date), a little patience and a whole lot of whisking and your meringues will turn out perfectly every time. The addition of cornflour makes the meringues more chewy, which is customary for pavlova-type meringues, but leave it out if you prefer.

Preheat the oven to its lowest setting. Wipe the inside of a large bowl and the whisk with the cut side of the lemon. This eliminates any last specks of unseen grease, which is a good idea.

Put the egg whites into this bowl, then whisk them until they begin to thicken and turn opaque – this will take a couple of minutes with a hand-held electric whisk or a little longer if you're using a balloon whisk and doing it by hand.

Add one-quarter of the sugar and whisk the egg whites again until the mixture goes stiff. Keep whisking the egg whites, and with the other hand, add the sugar in a thin, steady stream, whisking all the time. This technique is called 'meringuing the foam' and is a quick and easy way to make beautiful meringue.

When you have added all of the sugar, keep whisking the meringue until all the mixture is really stiff and shiny. To check that it's ready, take some of the meringue on the end of the whisk, then turn the whisk meringue-covered end up – the meringue should be super stiff and not at all floppy. If you want a slightly more soft, pavlova-like meringue, then fold in the cornflour along with any other spices or flavourings, such as toasted flaked almonds or finely grated lime rind, but I think they are perfect just as they are. →

Dab little blobs of the meringue under each corner of two large baking sheets lined with non-stick baking paper. The meringue will act like glue, stopping your paper from flying around in the oven. Take a big metal spoon and put 16 even-sized blobs of the mixture on the lined baking sheets. Sometimes I like to use a mechanical ice cream scoop, as I can get them to all be a pretty much similar size with ease. Leave a bit of room around each one because they will increase in size in the oven as they dry out. If you want a more pavlova-like shape, then use a smaller spoon to make a well in the centre of each one to make a cup or nest. Once baked, the whipped cream and fruit will sit in here.

Bake the meringues for 6 hours – you don't so much cook the meringues as dry them out. This method has the added benefit of keeping them snowy white. When they are ready, they should be crisp on the outside and sound hollow when tapped on the bottom. Once baked, turn off the oven and use a wooden spoon to keep the oven door open a crack to let any excess moisture out. Leave them in the oven to cool down completely, then transfer to an airtight container until needed.

To serve, top each meringue with a dollop of whipped cream, then add a few fresh berries or sliced summer fruits and decorate with a tiny mint sprig.

NEVEN'S TOP TIP

Separate the eggs one at a time into a ramekin before you tip them into the bowl that has been wiped with the lemon, being careful not to drop any egg yolk into the white. If you accidently drop any bits of shell into the ramekin, scoop them out with a spoon rather than using your fingers.

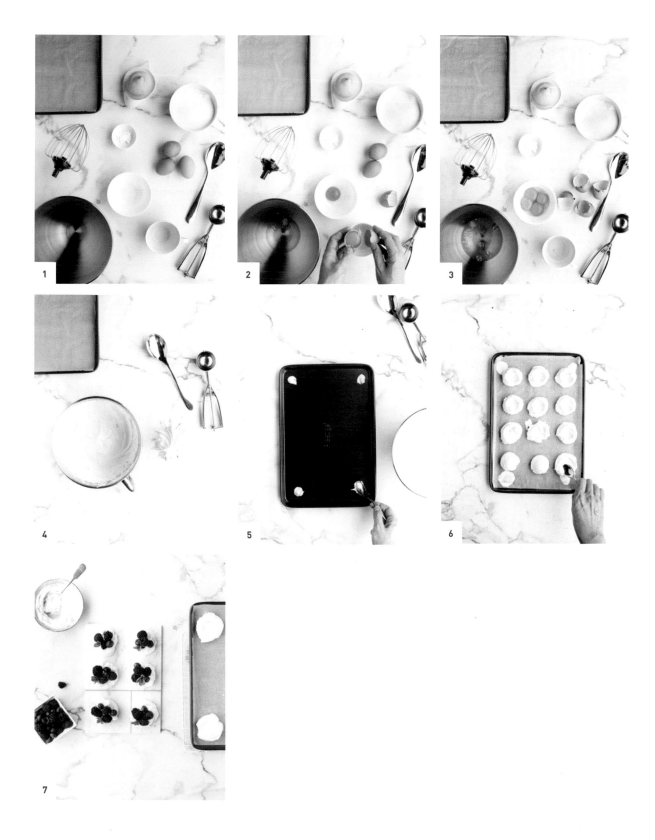

INDEX